Fathers of Confederation

Grades 4-8

Written by Frances Stanford
Illustrated by S&S Learning Materials & Ric Ward

ISBN 1-55035-723-9
Fathers of Confederation, SSJ1-45
Copyright 2002 S&S Learning Materials
Revised Feb. 2003
15 Dairy Avenue
Napanee, Ontario
K7R 1M4
All Rights Reserved * Printed in Canada
A Division of the Solski Group

Permission to Reproduce

Permission is granted to the individual teacher who purchases one copy of this book to reproduce the student activity material for use in his/her classroom only. Reproduction of these materials for an entire school or for a school system, or for other colleagues or for commercial sale is **strictly prohibited**. No part of this publication may be transmitted in any form or by any means, electronic, mechanical, recording or otherwise without the prior written permission of the publisher. "We acknowledge the financial support of the Government of Canada through the Book Publishing Industry Development program for our publishing activities."

Published in Canada by:
S&S Learning Materials
15 Dairy Avenue
Napanee, Ontario
K7R 1M4
www.sslearning.com

Published in the United States by:
T4T Learning Materials
3909 Witmer Road PMB 175
Niagara Falls, New York
14305
www.t4tlearning.com

© S&S Learning Materials

Look For OTHER CANADIAN UNITS

Item #SSJ1-01	Canada	Gr. 1
J1-02	All About Canada	2
J1-03	Let's Visit Canada	3
J1-04	Canadian Provinces	3-6
J1-11	Wild Animals of Canada	2-3
J1-12	Famous Canadians	4-8
J1-13	Let's Look at Canada	4-6
J1-23	Ottawa	7-9
J1-32	What is Canada?	P-K
J1-33	Canadian Capital Cities	4-6
J1-35	Toronto	4-8
J1-37	Canadian Arctic Inuit	2-3
J1-38	Canadian Provinces and Territories	4-6
J1-39	Canadian Government	5-8
J1-40	Development of Western Canada	7-8
J1-41	Canada and Its Trading Partners	6-8
J1-42	Canada's Traditions and Celebrations	1-3
J1-45	Fathers of Confederation	4-8
J1-47	Prime Ministers of Canada	4-8
J1-48	Canada's Landmarks	4-6

Let's Visit...

J1-14	Let's Visit Saskatchewan	2-4
J1-15	Let's Visit British Columbia	2-4
J1-16	Let's Visit Alberta	2-4
J1-17	Let's Visit Ontario	2-4
J1-18	Let's Visit Manitoba	2-4
J1-19	Let's Visit Prince Edward Island	2-4
J1-20	Let's Visit Nova Scotia	2-4
J1-21	Let's Visit New Brunswick	2-4
J1-27	Let's Visit Newfoundland and Labrador	2-4
J1-28	Let's Visit Yukon Territory	2-4
J1-30	Let's Visit Northwest Territory	2-4
J1-31	Let's Visit Québec	2-4
J1-34	Let's Visit Nunavut	2-4

Discover Canada

J1-22	Discover Québec	5-7
J1-24	Discover Prince Edward Island	5-7
J1-25	Discover Ontario	5-7
J1-26	Discover Nova Scotia	5-7
J1-36	Discover Nunavut Territory	5-7

Canadian Communities

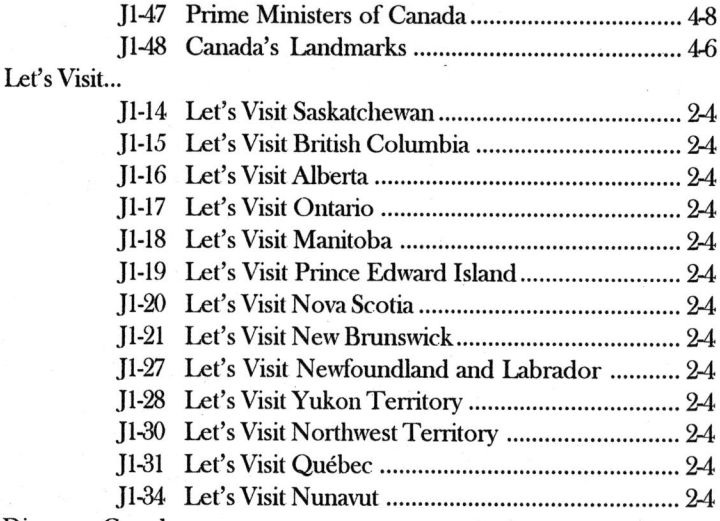

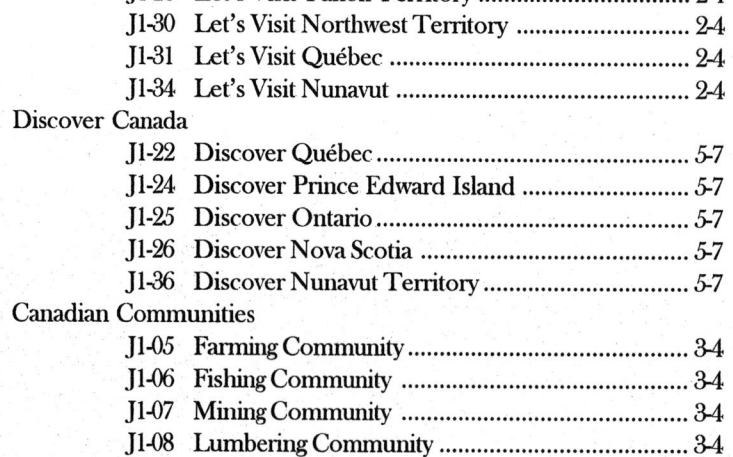

J1-05	Farming Community	3-4
J1-06	Fishing Community	3-4
J1-07	Mining Community	3-4
J1-08	Lumbering Community	3-4
J1-09	Ranching Community	3-4
J1-10	Inuit Community	3-4

Published by:
S&S Learning Materials
15 Dairy Avenue
Napanee, Ontario
K7R 1M4

All rights reserved.
Printed in Canada.

Distributed in U.S.A. by:
T4T Learning Materials
3909 Witmer Road PMB 175
Niagara Falls, New York
14305

© S&S Learning Materials

Fathers of Confederation

Table of Contents

Learning Outcomes	4
Teacher Input Suggestions	5
List of Resources	5
List of Vocabulary	6
Introduction	7
Sir John A. Macdonald	11
George Brown	14
Sir Adams George Archibald	16
Sir Alexander Campbell and Sir Frederic Carter	18
Sir George-Étienne Cartier and Edward Barron Chandler	22
Jean-Charles Chapais and George Coles	25
James Cockburn, Robert Barry Dickey and Charles Fisher	28
Sir Alexander T. Galt	31
(Lt. Col.) John Hamilton Gray, John Hamilton Gray and Thomas Heath Haviland	33
William Alexander Henry, Sir William Pearce Howland and John Mercer Johnson	37
Sir Hector-Louis Langevin, Andrew Archibald MacDonald and Jonathan McCully	40
William McDougall	43
Thomas D'Arcy McGee	45
Peter Mitchell and Sir Oliver Mowat	47
Edward Palmer	50
William Henry Pope	52
John William Ritchie and Sir Ambrose Shea	54
William Henry Steeves and Sir Étienne-Paschal Tache	57
Sir Samuel Leonard Tilley and Sir Charles Tupper	60
Edward Whelan and Robert Ducan Wilmot	64
Who Were They?	67
Quiz 1	71
Quiz 2	73
Answer Key	76

Fathers of Confederation

Learning Outcomes

At the end of this unit of study, the students will:
- understand the meaning of the term "Fathers of Confederation"
- know who the Fathers of Canadian Confederation were and what they did
- understand the reasons for their actions
- demonstrate knowledge of the political situation in Canada at the time of Confederation
- be able to analyse the reasons used for forming a union of British North American colonies
- understand the significance of Confederation on their own lives

Bulletin Board Ideas

On a bulletin board make a display of any of the following:
- a map of Canada before Confederation
- a recent map of Canada showing the provinces and territories
- pictures of the Quebec and Charlottetown Conferences
- pictures of the Fathers of Confederation
- a timeline of entry into Confederation of the various provinces and territories

Guest Speakers

1. Make sure that you contact a guest speaker such as a representative of the provincial or federal government well in advance of this topic to ensure that they are available to visit your classroom.

2. Have the students prepare their questions or inquiries well in advance and discuss the questions to ensure they are appropriate for the occasion.

3. Send a newsletter home with the students to inform parents about the upcoming unit of study. Include an invitation to the parents to come to the class as many of them may be able to speak to the class on aspects of this topic.

Fathers of Confederation

Teaching Suggestions

Collect any of the following prior to beginning this unit:
- reference books and material pertaining to the Fathers of Confederation
- pamphlets about the Fathers of Confederation
- pictures of the Fathers of Confederation at the Quebec and Charlottetown Conferences
- political cartoons regarding Confederation
- copies of the British North America Act, the Seventy-Two Resolutions and the new Canadian Constitution
- collections of songs regarding Confederation
- copies of speeches made by the Fathers of Confederation

Teachers should read this book before beginning any work on the unit with their classes.

This unit can be used in conjunction with the units on "Confederation", "The Development of Western Canada" or "Our Canadian Governments".

As a culminating activity, students could prepare their own version of the Charlottetown and Quebec Conferences complete with appropriate dress and speeches.

List of Resources

Bliss, Michael,	**Confederation; A New Nationality**
Ford, Karen,	**Great Canadian Lives**
Lunn, Janet,	**The Story of Canada**
Schull, Joseph,	**The Nation Makers**
	The Junior Encyclopedia of Canada
	The Encyclopedia of Newfoundland and Labrador
Hayes, John,	**The Nation Builders**
Stephenson, William,	**Dawn of the Nation**

Fathers of Confederation

List of Vocabulary

Charlottetown Conference, Quebec Conference, Seventy-Two Resolutions, Fenian Raids, Reciprocity Treaty, London Conference, British North America Act, Dominion of Canada, Fathers of Confederation, Province of Canada, responsible government, representation by population, Placeman's Bill, French Convention, Labouchere Dispatch, French Shore Question, Louis Joseph Papineau, Rebellion of 1837, Fils de la Liberte, St-Jean Baptiste Society, Intercolonial Railway, Grand Trunk Railway, seigneurial system, Order in Council, texian fever, Absentee Landlord Question, Tenant League, Smashers, Prohibition, Rummies, Temperance, Canada Company, British North American Land Company, Separatist Movement, Montgomery's Tavern, suffrage, secularization of the clergy, Hincks - Monn coalition, Wandering Willie, Rupert's Land, Hudson's Bay Company, Canadian Visit, status quo, Better Terms, nondepartmentalism, patronage, Confederate Council on Commercial Treaties, Act of Union, Draper - Papineau government, LaFontaine - Baldwin government, Patriot, Parti Rouge, National Policy, Canadian Pacific Railway, Welland Canal, secessionism, William Fielding, Joseph Howe, Boer War, Pacific Scandal.

Websites

http://collections.ic.gc.ca/charlottetown/
http://www.hpedsb.on.ca/coll/Fathers/

Fathers of Confederation

Introduction

Before 1867, the only independent nation in North America was the United States. Canada, as we know it today, did not exist. It consisted of a group of British colonies that were dependent upon Britain, and had very little contact with each other. The colonies on the Atlantic coast were Newfoundland, Nova Scotia, New Brunswick and Prince Edward Island. The inland colonies were Upper and Lower Canada, which became the Province of Canada consisting of Canada East and Canada West in 1841. The rest of the country was unsettled, except by the Natives, and was owned by the Hudson's Bay Company who called it Rupert's Land. Each of these colonies had developed its own way of life based on fishing, farming, lumbering and fur trading.

When Britain created the Province of Canada in 1841, it had done so with the hope that the English speaking population of Canada West would overcome the French speaking population of Canada East and bring an end to the use of French. This attempt failed because of the skill gained in politics by the French. It also failed to provide good government to the colony. Both parts of the province had equal representation in the Legislature and disputes often became bitter. Two political parties emerged: the Conservatives of Canada East called the "Bleus" and the Reformers of Canada West called the "Rouges". By the late 1850's, the government had almost come to a standstill and consequently, no one party could hold power for very long.

By the 1860's, the politicians had come to the conclusion that this form of government was not working. Their determination to change the system was the beginning of Confederation. The deadlock within the government in the province of Canada forced two political enemies - John A. Macdonald and George Brown - to form a coalition government. The main idea behind this coalition was to unite all the British North American colonies. At the same time, several situations arose that seemed to give the idea of Confederation a push. The Canadians realized that there was a possibility of the United States trying to annex Canada as a part of its country. Britain had started to buy its products from other countries and not just from the British North American colonies. Railways had come to British North America in the 1850's and had begun to change the way of life of the colonists, bringing them closer together with the other colonies.

Fathers of Confederation

In 1864 the colonial governments of the Atlantic colonies, Nova Scotia, New Brunswick, Prince Edward Island, and Newfoundland, decided to have a meeting in Charlottetown, Prince Edward Island to discuss the possibility of forming a union of these four colonies. The politicians from the Province of Canada heard about the upcoming meeting. They asked if they could attend and were accepted. As a result of this meeting, the representatives from the Atlantic Provinces decided to put aside their original plans and work towards forming a Confederation of all the British colonies in North America. They decided that they would unite under one central government, which would give power to the nation as a whole. Each colony would become a province of this central government with powers to deal with its own individual matters. As part of the plan, the central government would build a railway to connect the colonies. This was the first in a series of meetings to formulate the Confederation proposal and is known as the **Charlottetown Conference**.

The second meeting was held in Quebec and is known as the **Quebec Conference**. It was attended by delegates from Nova Scotia, New Brunswick, Prince Edward Island and the United Province of Canada: Canada East and Canada West. Newfoundland sent two observers, since it had not made a firm commitment to join the Confederation. The objective of this meeting was to work out the details of the union of the colonies. George Brown insisted on **representation by population**, since it would give his home province, Canada West, the majority in the government. The Maritime Provinces started to lose interest. Prince Edward Island decided not to join, since a railway to the Atlantic Provinces would be of little benefit to them. However, an agreement was worked out that the four colonies of Canada East, Canada West, Nova Scotia and New Brunswick would pursue the idea of forming a union. The agreement included seventy-two points on which the delegates agreed and is known as the **Seventy-Two Resolutions**.

When the resolutions from the conference were brought back to each colonial government, there were strong objections to Confederation. Canada West opposed the building of a railway, while the French speaking voters of Canada East thought they would be even further oppressed by the English speaking majority. In the Maritimes, the issue was attacked in the newspapers and used as an election issue. Leonard Tilley of New Brunswick lost his seat in the government because he was one of the delegates who had supported Confederation. However, the British were delighted with the idea of a union of the colonies. They were finding that the cost of defending the colonies was becoming too expensive. They sent a new governor to ensure that Tilley was elected back into office. The **Fenian Raids** from the United States, which introduced a new threat of being taken over by the Americans, and the end of the **Reciprocity Treaty** with the United States, helped to overcome the objections to Confederation.

Fathers of Confederation

A third conference was held in London, England in March 1867. It was at this **London Conference** that the actual details of Confederation were worked out. The British Parliament passed the **British North America Act** which established Canada as a nation called the **Dominion of Canada**. This act became law on July 1, 1867, with Sir John A. Macdonald as its first Prime Minister.

Fathers of Confederation

The term **Fathers of Confederation** refers to the names of the delegates who attended the Charlottetown, Quebec and London Conferences at which Canadian Confederation was planned and established.

Canadian Provinces and Territories and Dates of Joining

Quebec, Ontario, Nova Scotia, New Brunswick	1867
Manitoba, Northwest Territories	1870
British Columbia	1871
Prince Edward Island	1873
Yukon Territory	1898
Saskatchewan, Alberta	1905
Newfoundland	1949
Nunavut Territory (separate from the Northwest Territories)	2000

The Fathers of Confederation   *Introduction*

Name: _____ **Date:** _____

Points to Ponder

1. What were the forces that led politicians to call a meeting in Charlottetown in 1864? Why did the politicians from the Province of Canada want to attend?

   _____
   _____
   _____
   _____

2. What was the result of the Quebec Conference?

   _____
   _____

3. What did the British government think of the idea of a confederation of the colonies in British North America? Why?

   _____
   _____

4. What was the result of the London Conference?

   _____
   _____

5. What does the term "Fathers of Confederation" mean?

   _____
   _____

🍁🍁 Explore History 🍁🍁

1. What were the Seventy-Two Resolutions? Research this topic and prepare a poster for your class.

2. What is the motto of Canada? Why is this appropriate?

3. Draw a timeline showing the dates of entry into Confederation for all parts of Canada.

4. Why was Canada given the name "Dominion of Canada"?

© S&S Learning Materials

Fathers of Confederation

Sir John A. Macdonald (1815 - 1891)

John A. Macdonald was born on January 11, 1815 in Glasgow, Scotland. He moved to Kingston, Upper Canada with his family when he was only five years old. His mother insisted that John should have a proper education and he was sent to the Midland Grammar School in Kingston. He later attended a smaller school operated by a clergyman from Scotland. At the age of fifteen, he was apprenticed to a Kingston lawyer named George Mackenzie. By the time Macdonald was eighteen, Mackenzie regarded him with such admiration that he sent him to open a law office in Napanee. The following year, he took over the practice of a relative in Hallowell and when Mackenzie died in 1835, MacDonald returned to Kingston to start his own legal practice. He was called to the bar a year later.

His legal reputation grew steadily based on a succession of small cases rather than on any one large case. By 1842, his law practice had become one of the busiest in Canada. In 1843, he began his long career as a politician by becoming an alderman on the Kingston Town Council. In 1844, he ran for a seat in the Legislative Assembly of the **Province of Canada,** which consisted of the two former colonies of Canada West (Upper Canada) and Canada East (Lower Canada). He won his seat by a large majority.

From the beginning, Macdonald was a Conservative. He opposed the power of the ruling class, the Family Compact, and helped to build the power of a more moderate group, the Liberal Conservative party, which later became the Progressive Conservative party. Even though his party lost its majority in the election of 1848, Macdonald was one of the few Conservatives to be re-elected. He did not take part in any of the protests and rebellions that occurred during 1837, choosing instead to work to broaden the party base. He even decided to work with his enemies, the French Canadian politicians. He worked with George Brown, the leader of the Grits (later to become the Liberal Party), to defeat the Reform government in the election of 1854.

In the government of 1854, Macdonald served as Attorney General deciding against becoming Premier in favour of Étienne Tache, as it was important to retain the French votes in Canada East. In 1858, when a law was passed to make Ottawa the official capital of the Province of Canada, George Brown defeated the government on this issue. He became Premier, but this only lasted for a few days. For the next few years, the government seesawed back and forth between the two political parties reaching a political impasse in 1864. At this time, a coalition government was formed called the Tache-Macdonald government. George Brown agreed to join the government on the condition that it would work towards a federal union of all the British North American colonies. Macdonald was not in favor of such a union, but he agreed so that some sense of order could be restored to the government. He may have been slow to accept the possibility of Confederation, but once he did, he made it his own personal goal.

Fathers of Confederation

Macdonald's Role in Confederation

The Maritime colonies were considering the possibility of forming their own union and planned a meeting in Charlottetown, Prince Edward Island for September 1, 1864. Macdonald heard about the upcoming conference and requested permission for the Province of Canada to send a delegation. The Maritimers agreed and decided to put off their own discussion until they heard what the Canadians had to say. At this meeting, John A. Macdonald took the lead, pointing out the advantages of a confederation of all the colonies. He helped to draft the Seventy-Two Resolutions and also took the lead at the Quebec Conference in the same year. It was Macdonald who actually wrote the **British North America Act** (the Canadian Constitution) making Canada a federal nation with two levels of government - federal and provincial - and outlined how the system was to work. His aim was to give Canada a federal system with a strong central government and executive. This is the same constitution, with a few amendments, that Canada still has today.

When the Act became law on July 1, 1867, Macdonald became the first Prime Minister of Canada. He remained in power until 1873, but was returned as Prime Minister in 1878. He served in this position until his death in 1891. During his terms of office, he worked to make the dream of Canada a nation from sea to sea. He brought Manitoba, Prince Edward Island and British Columbia into the Confederation. He oversaw the building of the Canadian Pacific Railway to link British Columbia with the rest of Canada. He is known as the father and founder of Canada.

The Fathers of Confederation　　　　　　　　　　　*Sir John A. MacDonald*

Name: _____　　**Date:** _____

Points to Ponder

1. How did Macdonald gain experience as a lawyer?
   _____
   _____
   _____

2. What did he do instead of taking part in the Rebellions of 1837?
   _____
   _____

3. Why did he form a coalition government with George Brown?
   _____
   _____

4. Why was he in favour of Étienne Tache becoming Premier instead of taking the job himself?
   _____
   _____

5. Why did he change his mind and decide to support the idea of Confederation?
   _____
   _____

🍁🍁 Explore History 🍁🍁

1. What were the Rebellions of 1837? Who were the leaders? Why were they dissatisfied with the government?

2. Research the Canadian Constitution. How is it different today from when it was first written?

3. Macdonald's government was put out of power in 1873 because of the Pacific Scandal. What was this about? Why did it affect the government?

© S&S Learning Materials　　　　SSJ1-45

Fathers of Confederation

George Brown (1818 - 1880)

George Brown was born on November 29, 1818 in Alloa, Scotland and was educated in Edinburgh. At age twenty, he emigrated to New York and later moved to Toronto, where he founded the *Globe* as a weekly newspaper in 1844, and as a daily newspaper in 1853. He was a vigorous writer and a strong Presbyterian. He opposed all church affiliated schools, especially those run by the Roman Catholic Church. He was elected to the Legislative Assembly of the Province of Canada in 1851 and was the leader of the Reform (Liberal) Party of Canada West. For years, he used his newspaper to promote the Reform Party and its advocation of **responsible government.** He also used the paper as a way to preach the idea of settling and colonizing the West.

George Brown hated the Catholics and anything that he viewed as being anti-British. As a member of the Legislative Assembly for the Province of Canada and a representative for Canada West, he argued for **representation by population** in the Assembly. The two provinces of Canada East and Canada West had been given equal representation in the Assembly, but Brown realized that his "rep by pop" would give Canada West a bigger majority in the Assembly. He found it very difficult to accept the Conservative push for a federal union of the two provinces. He argued for a union of Upper and Lower Canada which would be a federation that would create two separate provinces.

Most of all, Brown hated John A. Macdonald, his political rival in the Assembly. The two men flung insults at each other in the Assembly and did everything possible to thwart the actions of each other. The quarreling between the two leaders reached a political deadlock in the government, and it seemed that there was no solution. In June, 1864, Brown made a startling offer in the Legislature. He agreed to work with the opposition on one condition: that they work towards a common cause: the transformation of British North America into one nation. There would be no more squabbling in the Legislature and they could get on with doing the government work they were supposed to be doing. Macdonald and Cartier agreed to work with Brown. It is said that through this, Macdonald and Brown made "the most important handshake in Canadian history".

Brown was a delegate to the Charlottetown and Quebec Conferences. He worked hard at developing a plan for Confederation. It was Brown who designed the plan for the federal-provincial system that became the basis for Canadian Confederation. This system is still in use today.

Once Brown realized his dream of attaining a Confederation for Canada, he resigned from politics. However, he continued to shape his ideas through the newspaper. On March 25, 1880, at the age of sixty-one, he was shot by a disgruntled employee who had been dismissed from the newspaper. He lingered near death, until he finally died on May 9 of the same year.

The Fathers of Confederation George Brown

Name: _____ **Date:** _____

Points to Ponder

1. How did Brown's newspaper help him to advocate his political views?

2. Do you agree with the way Brown used his paper to publicize his political views? Why or why not?

3. Why did Brown decide to cooperate with his political opponents?

4. What part did Brown play in the formation of Confederation?

5. Why do you think he resigned from politics?

🍁🍁 Explore History 🍁🍁

1. Research the statistics of the number of voters in Canada East and Canada West in the 1860's. How would **representation by population** have benefitted Canada West? What would the division of seats have been for each province?

2. What is **responsible government**? How is it the same or different from the system of government we enjoy today?

Fathers of Confederation

Sir Adams George Archibald (1814 - 1892)

Adams George Archibald was born on May 18, 1814 in Truro, Nova Scotia. He attended the local school in Truro and received his higher education at Pictou Academy in Pictou, Nova Scotia. He originally intended to study medicine to become a doctor, but changed his mind and studied law in Prince Edward Island. In 1838, he was called to the bar of Prince Edward Island and in 1839, to the bar of Nova Scotia. He returned to Truro and set up his own law practice.

In 1851, Archibald became involved in Nova Scotia's struggle to attain responsible government. He left his law practice and entered politics. He represented the electoral district of Colchester County in the Nova Scotia House of Assembly from that time until 1867. During that period, he was appointed to the position of Solicitor General in 1856 and to the position of Attorney General in 1860. He succeeded Joseph Howe as leader of the party in 1863.

He was invited by Charles Tupper to be a delegate at the Charlottetown Conference of September 1864. He was a strong supporter of Confederation and went on to attend the later conferences in Quebec and London. As the financial expert at the conferences, it was his job to justify the financial arrangements of Confederation to the people of Nova Scotia. He defended Confederation against the strong criticisms of Joseph Howe and William Annand. He became Canada's first Secretary of State on July 1, 1867, but was defeated in the next general election. In 1869, he was re-elected as the federal representative of Colchester County, but resigned in 1870 to accept the position of Lieutenant Governor of Manitoba and the Northwest Territories. He was seen as an able candidate for this position as he was bilingual and from the Maritimes, which would not be seen as favoring either the French or English speaking people of the area.

In this position, he established the basis for the civil institutions of Manitoba and the Northwest Territories, such as schools and court systems. He negotiated the first two treaties with the Native People of Canada. He received a knighthood from the Queen for his work as Lieutenant Governor.

On June 24, 1873, he was appointed Judge of Equity for the province of Nova Scotia and replaced Joseph Howe as Lieutenant Governor of the province on July 4 of the same year. He remained in this position until 1883. In 1888, he was once again elected to the House of Commons as the representative for Colchester County, which he held until his retirement from politics in 1891. He died in Truro, Nova Scotia on December 14, 1892.

The Fathers of Confederation   *Sir Adams George Archibald*

Name: _____ **Date:** _____

Points to Ponder

1. What did Archibald do to persuade voters to accept the idea of Confederation in Nova Scotia?
   _____
   _____

2. What did he achieve in the position of Lieutenant Governor of Manitoba and the Northwest Territories?
   _____
   _____

3. How did Archibald demonstrate that he was committed to the political cause of attaining responsible government for Nova Scotia?
   _____
   _____

4. What qualities did he possess to be appointed to the position of Lieutenant Governor in Manitoba? Why were these qualities important?
   _____
   _____
   _____

🍁🍁 Explore History 🍁🍁

1. What were the Terms of Union by which Nova Scotia would enter Confederation? What finances were involved in this, that Archibald would have to justify to Nova Scotia voters?

2. What is a Lieutenant Governor? What is involved in working in this position?

3. Who is the Lieutenant Governor of your province? What does he/she do?

4. What two treaties did Archibald negotiate with the Native People of Canada? Why were these important?

Fathers of Confederation

Sir Alexander Campbell (1822 - 1892)

Alexander Campbell was born on March 9, 1822 in Hedon, Yorkshire, England. He was brought to Canada by his father when he was a year old. He received his education at Kingston Grammar School and St. Hyacinthe College. He studied law and shortly after being called to the bar, he became a law partner of John A. Macdonald.

Campbell was elected to the Legislative Council as the representative for Cataraqui (now Kingston and the Islands) in 1858. In 1867, he was made Commissioner of Crown Lands and was a delegate to the Charlottetown and Quebec Conferences on Confederation. He was considered by John A. Macdonald to be a great organizer.

After Confederation, he was made Postmaster General in Macdonald's first Cabinet. He no longer ran for election to government after 1867, but he did hold a variety of positions in the Conservative government: Postmaster General from 1867 - 1873, 1879 - 1881, 1885 - 1887; Minister of the Interior in 1873; Receiver General from 1878 - 1879; Minister of Militia in 1880 and Minister of Justice from 1881 - 1885.

He was appointed to the Senate in 1867. He acted as government leader from 1867 to 1873 and leader of the opposition from 1873 to 1878 when he returned as government leader until 1887. In 1887, he left the Senate to become the Lieutenant Governor of Ontario and represented Canada at the first colonial conference. He died on May 24, 1892 in Toronto.

© S&S Learning Materials

SSJ1-45

Fathers of Confederation

Sir Frederic Carter (1819 - 1900)

Frederic Bowker Terrington Carter was born on February 12, 1819 in St. John's, Newfoundland. When he was only ten years old, he received the first of many honours to be bestowed upon him during his lifetime. As a student, he was awarded prizes for declamation, recitation, writing and English grammar. He studied law under Sir Bryan Robinson and became a lawyer in 1840. He went to London to continue his studies in Constitutional law and returned to Newfoundland in 1842. He then went into private practice. In 1848, he was appointed to the position of Solicitor to the House of Assembly. He remained in that position until 1852. In 1854, he was appointed Judge of the Supreme Court during the illness of Judge Augustus des Barres.

Newfoundland was granted responsible government in 1855 and in the election which followed Carter was elected as a Conservative in the district of Trinity. As a member of the opposition, he introduced many measures and spoke at length on a variety of issues. In 1856, he introduced the **Placeman's Bill** which attempted to place restrictions on who could be elected to the House of Assembly. The bill was voted down. Carter re-introduced the bill on three more occasions and each time it was defeated.

In January 1858, the British government signed an agreement with France called the **French Convention**. This bill gave French fishermen rights to fish along the French Shore of Newfoundland as well as five harbours on the west coast and other concessions. Newfoundland protested the convention. Frederic Carter went to Nova Scotia, New Brunswick and the Province of Canada to speak in the legislatures trying to enlist the help of the other colonies in protesting the convention. They were successful and the convention was dropped. The result was the **Labouchere Dispatch** which guaranteed the independence of Colonial legislatures.

Carter became Speaker of the Assembly in 1861 and he re-introduced his Placeman's Bill. This time he was successful in getting the bill added to the laws of Newfoundland. He also helped prepare necessary legislation for the adoption and adaptation of the procedures of English common law to the Newfoundland judicial system.

There were no Newfoundland delegates at the Charlottetown Conference. However, they were invited to send two delegates to the Quebec Conference. The Newfoundland delegates were Frederic Carter and Ambrose Shea. They had no power to commit Newfoundland to joining Confederation and were there as observers, only to act as onlookers and report back to the House of Assembly. They returned convinced that Newfoundland would benefit from being a partner in the Confederation of the colonies. When Confederation became a reality in 1867, Carter stood by

Fathers of Confederation

his promise not to bring Newfoundland into the union without consulting the people of the colony in a general election. He felt that the people should be made familiar with the options available to them and be given ample time to decide the issue. Carter brought the issue of Confederation with Canada to the voters in the election of 1869 and was soundly defeated. The anti-Confederates, under Charles Bennett, convinced the voters that Newfoundland would be much better off on its own. He himself was defeated but was re-elected to the Assembly in the district of Burin in 1870 and entered the House as the Leader of the Opposition. Confederation was not raised as an issue in the following elections.

Carter's party was returned to power in 1874, when the most pressing issue for his administration was the **French Shore Question**. He went to England in an attempt to clarify Newfoundland's jurisdiction in the problem. The result of his negotiations was that the colony was now allowed to appoint magistrates, customs collectors and other public officials and hold elections for representation in the House of Assembly from the area formerly known as the French Shore. Carter resigned as Prime Minister of Newfoundland in 1878 when he was appointed to the Newfoundland Supreme Court. He received a knighthood from the Queen in that year as well. He has been called "The Grand Old Man" of Newfoundland politics.

The Fathers of Confederation   *Campbell and Carter*

Name: _____ **Date:** _____

Points to Ponder

1. Why do you think Macdonald asked Alexander Campbell to be a delegate to the conferences to discuss Confederation?

   _____
   _____
   _____

2. What part did Frederic Carter play in the Quebec Conference?

   _____
   _____

3. Why didn't Newfoundland join Confederation in 1867? In 1869?

   _____
   _____
   _____

4. Why didn't Carter resurrect the Confederation issue when he returned to power in 1874?

   _____
   _____
   _____

🍁🍁 *Explore History* 🍁🍁

1. What was the **French Shore Question** in Newfoundland history? How was it resolved?

2. What was the **Placeman's Bill**? Is it still law in Newfoundland?

3. What was the **Labouchere Dispatch**?

4. Alexander Campbell represented Canada at the first colonial conference. Where and when was this conference held? What was decided?

Fathers of Confederation

Sir George-Étienne Cartier (1814 - 1873)

George-Étienne Cartier was born on September 6, 1814 in St. Antoine, Lower Canada. He grew up in the Richelieu Valley and was educated at the Sulpician's College in Montreal. He trained as a lawyer and opened his own law office in Montreal in 1835. He allied himself with Louis-Joseph Papineau to fight for the rights of the French speaking people of Lower Canada and took part in the **Rebellion of 1837**. He fought in the Battle of St. Denis, but when the uprising failed, he escaped to Vermont. He was a member of the radical group, **Fils de la Liberte**, and secretary of the **St-Jean Baptiste Society**. He returned to Montreal in 1848, re-opened his law office and entered politics.

In 1848, he was elected to the Legislature of Canada East as a Conservative member. He represented Vercheres from 1848 to 1861 and Montreal East from 1861 to 1872 with the union of Upper and Lower Canada. He became a strong supporter of John A. Macdonald and the Confederation cause, and served as joint head of government with Macdonald from 1858 to 1861. Therefore, it was only natural that Macdonald would invite him to be one of the delegates to the Charlottetown Conference.

It was largely through the efforts of Cartier that French Canadians came to accept Confederation. He believed that French Canada could better protect its distinct culture within a federation than in the existing union. The trust the voters had in him was a vital factor in the achievement of Confederation. He participated in all three conferences and devoted a tremendous amount of time to the cause between 1864 and 1867. After Confederation, he became the Minister of Militia in Macdonald's Cabinet handling such important details as the entry of British Columbia into Confederation, the purchasing of Rupert's Land from the Hudson's Bay Company, and supporting the building of the **Grand Trunk Railway** and the **Canadian Pacific Railway**. He codified the civil law of Quebec which brought an end to the oppressive seigneurial tenure in the province. It was Cartier who gave the contract to build the Canadian Pacific Railway to Sir Hugh Allan and received $85,000.00 as campaign funds in return. This looked so much like a bribe that it was the cause of the **Pacific Scandal**, which defeated the Macdonald government in 1873.

In 1872, he became embroiled in a dispute with the Bishop of Montreal. He lost the election, but took a Manitoba seat instead. By that time, he was ill with kidney disease for which there was no cure. He travelled to England, hoping to find a cure, but he died in London on May 20, 1873.

Fathers of Confederation

Edward Barron Chandler (1800 - 1880)

Edward Barron Chandler was born on August 22, 1800 in Amherst, Nova Scotia and received his early education there. He moved to New Brunswick to study law and was called to the bar in 1823. In 1827, he entered politics as the elected member for the County of Westmoreland. He held this seat until 1836. From 1844 to 1858, he served on the Executive Council. He was one of the earliest proponents of a railway to connect the Maritime colonies to the Province of Canada. In 1851 he went to Canada with Joseph Howe to secure an agreement to build the **Intercolonial Railway**. When guaranteed loans could not be found for this project, Nova Scotia and New Brunswick went ahead with it inside their own boundaries.

He supported Confederation and was a delegate for New Brunswick to the Charlottetown Conference. He supported the idea of Confederation in principle, but disliked the extensive power it gave to the central government. In 1862, the idea of an Intercolonial Railway was revived and this became one of the conditions on which the Maritimes would enter Confederation. Work was started in 1867 and because of his interest in the project from the beginning, Chandler was made Commissioner in charge of the construction.

After Confederation, he was offered a seat in the Canadian Senate, but declined preferring instead to remain in provincial politics. In 1878, he became Lieutenant Governor of New Brunswick. He died two years later in Fredericton on February 6, 1880.

The Fathers of Confederation   *Cartier and Chandler*

Name: _____   **Date:** _____

Points to Ponder

1. How was Cartier instrumental in encouraging the French speaking voters to accept Confederation?

2. Why is it ironic that Cartier was made Minister of Militia in Macdonald's first Cabinet?

3. What part did Chandler play in building the Intercolonial Railway?

4. What important achievements were made by Cartier after Confederation?

5. How did Cartier cause the Pacific Scandal?

🍁🍁 Explore History 🍁🍁

1. Who was **Louis-Joseph Papineau**? Why did he rebel against the government of Lower Canada?

2. What part did he play in the Rebellion of 1837?

3. What was the **Battle of St. Denis**? What was the result of this battle?

4. When was the Intercolonial Railway built? Draw a map showing the route it took.

Fathers of Confederation

Jean-Charles Chapais (1811 - 1885)

Jean-Charles Chapais was born on December 2, 1811 in Riviere Ouelle, Quebec. He was educated at Nicolet College and Quebec Seminary. He followed in his father's footsteps to become a merchant. His family was one of the wealthy, politically active families that guided the development of the parish community of St. Denis. He was the first Mayor of St. Denis, while his father-in-law, Amable Dionne, served in the Colonial Legislature representing Kamouraska. It was through Dionne's encouragement that Chapais entered politics in 1851 with his election to the Kamouraska riding. In 1864, when Macdonald and Brown formed a coalition government, Chapais was named Commissioner of Public Works. It was in this position that he attended the Quebec Conference on Confederation. He established the Intercolonial Railway and developed the **Grand Trunk Railway**, which set the groundwork for Confederation.

In 1867, Chapais was named Canada's first Minister of Agriculture. The mandate of this portfolio included immigration and emigration, public health and quarantine, the marine and emigrant hospital at Quebec, arts and manufacturing, census, statistics and registrations, patents and copyrights as well as industrial designs and trademarks. At the same time, he held a seat in the Quebec provincial legislature. When he ran for the federal election for the Kamouraska seat, the result was indecisive and "no election" was declared. Rioting and a scandal over irregularities in voting meant that the riding lost its right to representation in the government for two years. In 1868, Chapais was named to the Senate and continued to hold the Agriculture portfolio until 1869 when he was named Receiver General.

While working as Minister of Agriculture, Chapais worked hard to reform the agricultural legislation, including the abolition of the **seigneurial system** in Quebec and the development of laws related to farming and settlement. His first recorded action was an **Order in Council** on August 13, 1868, prohibiting imports of horned cattle from the United States because of the threat of **texian fever**, which could contaminate livestock transported by rail. He was so dedicated to the cause of the French speaking people and the Catholic religion that Sir John A. Macdonald nicknamed him "My Little Nun".

Jean Chapais officially finished as an elected official in politics with the fall of the Macdonald government in 1873. However, he remained active in the Senate until his death in Ottawa on July 17, 1885.

Fathers of Confederation

George Coles (1810 - 1875)

George Coles was born on Prince Edward Island on September 20, 1810. He had very little formal schooling, but travelled to England when he was nineteen to learn about the brewing industry. While in England, he married Mercy Haine on August 14, 1833. The couple returned to Prince Edward Island that same year. Throughout his life, Coles had many jobs: merchant, brewer, steam mill operator, farm operator, landlord and politician. He was quite a colourful character and is said to have duelled with Edward Palmer and to have challenged James C. Pope to a duel as well.

In 1842, he ran for and was elected to the Legislative Assembly of Prince Edward Island. At first he claimed to be a Conservative, but he joined the Reformers in 1847 as he often found himself to be in conflict with the Conservative Party leadership. In 1846, he had to spend thirty-one days in the custody of the Sergeant-at-Arms for refusing to retract a statement he made in the assembly. He was a prominent figure in the push for Prince Edward Island to receive responsible government and became the first Premier of the Island under the new system of government in 1851. He held this post, with one brief interruption, until his government lost power in 1859. His government was plagued with the **Absentee Landlords Question**. He neither supported the landlords nor the **Tenant League**, a mass movement which pushed for the non-payment of rent.

In 1864, Coles was a delegate to the Charlottetown and Quebec Conferences. At first, he was in favour of Confederation, on the condition that the terms of union for the Island would include a solution to the Absentee Landlords Question. He later changed his mind when the offer to purchase foreign-owned land holdings was not made part of the discussions at the Quebec Conference. He returned to Prince Edward Island to lead the Liberals to victory on an anti-Confederate platform.

He became Premier of Prince Edward Island for a third term in 1867. However, at this time, Coles' prosperous business properties were burned in a great fire that swept Charlottetown. Coles believed that there were bands of firebugs roaming the Island who might return. He resigned from office in 1868, went into seclusion and eventually went insane. He died in Charlottetown on August 21, 1875.

The Fathers of Confederation   *Chapais and Coles*

Name: _____   **Date:** _____

Points to Ponder

1. What position did Chapais hold that allowed him to go to the Quebec Conference?
   _____
   _____

2. What did Chapais achieve while in office?
   _____
   _____

3. Why was the last election in Kamouaska declared a "no election" for Chapais?
   _____
   _____

4. Why did Coles withdraw his support from Confederation?
   _____
   _____

5. Why did Coles spend thirty-one days in custody while he was a member of the provincial government?
   _____
   _____

🍁🍁 *Explore History* 🍁🍁

1. Draw a map showing the route of the **Grand Trunk Railway**.

2. What was the **Absentee Landlords Question** of Prince Edward Island? How was it resolved?

3. What was the **texian fever** that caused a ban on importing cattle from the United States?

4. What is an **Order in Council**?

Fathers of Confederation

James Cockburn (1819 - 1883)

James Cockburn was born on February 13, 1819 in Berwick, England. He emigrated to Canada with his family when he was thirteen years old. The family settled in Toronto and James was educated at the Upper Canada College. By the age of twenty-seven, he was a lawyer with his own practice in Cobourg.

In 1861, he was elected to the Legislative Assembly as the representative for Northumberland County. In 1864, he was appointed to the position of Solicitor General and was asked to be a delegate to the Quebec Conference. He did not have much to say at the conference. However, while the delegates were taken on an extended tour of the Canadas, he used the opportunity to have a supper meeting for them in Cobourg.

When the first federal Parliament was chosen, he was unanimously chosen to be the Speaker of the House. This was a huge task, as the politicians of that day were very outspoken and insulted each other openly in Parliament. It was Cockburn's job to keep everything in order. He was able to restrain Sir John A. Macdonald and Thomas D'Arcy McGee and still managed to hold their respect for the seven years that he held this position until 1874. He showed patience, tact and even courage, and set a high standard for the Speakers of the House which have followed him since then. He was re-elected in 1878 and remained in Parliament until 1881. He died in Ottawa on August 14, 1883.

Robert Barry Dickey (1811 - 1903)

Robert Dickey was born on November 10, 1811 in Amherst, Nova Scotia. He was educated at Windsor Academy and Truro Grammar School, beginning his study of law at the age of fifteen. He became a lawyer in 1834, setting up his law office in his hometown. He was not particularly interested in politics, but he accepted an appointment to the Legislative Council on the advice of his good friend, Charles Tupper. In this capacity, he visited London twice as part of a delegation regarding the Intercolonial Railway. He acted as Consular Agent for the United States and as a director for the Nova Scotia Electric Telegraph Company. He was invited by Tupper to be the Conservative delegate to the Charlottetown Conference and later to the Quebec Conference.

Dickey went to the Quebec Conference as a supporter of Confederation. However, the speeches he heard there convinced him that it would not be a good thing for the Maritimes to join with the Province of Canada. He agreed with Coles and Chandler that too much power was being given to the federal government, and became the most outspoken Nova Scotian critic of the Quebec plan. He did support the general idea of Confederation and supported Tupper's idea for another conference to be held in London. He continued to oppose Confederation until a better system of subsidies was developed in 1866.

Fathers of Confederation

Charles Fisher

When the first federal elections were held, Dickey did not run for election. He accepted an appointment to the Senate. He took very little part in public affairs. He died on July 14, 1903 in Amherst, Nova Scotia at the age of ninety-three.

Charles Fisher (1808 - 1880)

Charles Fisher was born in Fredericton, New Brunswick on August 15, 1808. He was a member of the first graduating class of King's College, Fredericton (now the University of New Brunswick) in 1829. He went to London to study law and returned to New Brunswick in 1833 to set up his own law practice.

He was elected to the Legislature of New Brunswick in 1841 as the representative for the riding of York and kept this seat for the next thirty years in spite of the political turmoil of the colony. He quickly became a champion for the cause of responsible government. At this time, his ideas were not acceptable to the established upper class citizens who were satisfied with the government. He was not a polished speaker, being very blunt and was often looked upon as being "uncouth" in his speeches. He was a member of a committee that had to get the provincial laws arranged in good order.

Fisher became Premier of New Brunswick in 1851 as the leader of a reform party called the **Smashers** (Liberals). He resigned in 1856 when he was defeated on the **Prohibition** issue. **Temperance** was a strong issue in New Brunswick politics during this period. The Smashers were in favor of abstinence, prohibiting the sale of liquor, while the **Rummies** (Conservatives) were against the prohibition of alcohol. He resigned again in 1861 over a scandal regarding Crown Lands. He was a delegate to the Quebec Conference. Though he lost his seat in the general election of 1865, he regained it in a by-election six months later. He was a strong supporter of Confederation, and as Attorney General, went to London to assist in framing the British North America Act.

In 1867, he was re-elected to the Federal House of Commons in the riding of York, but resigned in 1868 to become a judge of the Supreme Court of New Brunswick. He died in Fredericton on December 8, 1880.

The Fathers of Confederation *Cockburn, Dickey, and Fisher*

Name: _____ **Date:** _____

Points to Ponder

1. Why do you think there is little information known about these three Fathers of Confederation?
   _____
   _____
   _____

2. Why was it a huge task for Cockburn to be Speaker of the House?
   _____
   _____

3. Why did Dickey change his mind about Confederation?
   _____
   _____

4. Why were Fisher's ideas about responsible government not acceptable in New Brunswick?
   _____
   _____

5. Why do you think the names "Smashers" and "Rummies" were given to the Liberals and Conservatives in New Brunswick?
   _____
   _____

🍁🍁 Explore History 🍁🍁

1. What was Prohibition? When was this law enforced? What has changed since then?

2. What are the duties of the Speaker of the House?

3. When did responsible government become a reality in New Brunswick? How did it come about?

Fathers of Confederation

Sir Alexander T. Galt (1817 - 1893)

Alexander Tilloch Galt was born on September 6, 1817 in London, England. He came to Canada in 1828 with the **Canada Company**, which was founded by his father, John Galt. This was a settlement company, active in the area around Lake Huron. Though the company failed, it laid the groundwork for the city of Guelph. Galt returned to Canada in 1835 as a clerk with a new company, the **British American Land Company**, based in Sherbrooke, Quebec. In 1840, he wrote a paper which documented the company's successes and failures. This document made such an impression in London that in 1843, he was made secretary of the company, and commissioner in 1844. He directed the affairs of the company and promoted the building of railroads.

In 1849, he was elected to the Legislature of the united Province of Canada. In 1849, he signed a manifesto which favoured the annexation of Canada by the United States saying that this would be the only way to preserve the Anglo-Saxon Protestant way of life in Canada. He began his political career as a Reformer, but was persuaded by John A. Macdonald to become a Conservative and support Confederation. Galt was truly a pioneer of Confederation. As early as 1858, he proposed a federation of the British North American colonies. In the planning years of the 1860's, he was responsible for the financial arrangements of Confederation. He wanted Canada to be in control of its own financial affairs. It is to Galt that Canadians owe the fact that their currency is in dollars and cents, rather than the British pounds and pence. He wanted to see complete separation of Britain from the colonies.

When the Brown-Dorian ministry fell in 1853, Galt was asked to form a new government. He suggested instead that Macdonald and Cartier form the government on the condition that they work towards Confederation. The three men travelled to England in 1858, to present their proposal to Queen Victoria who accepted it with polite indifference. The idea was shelved until 1863. Galt attended all three conferences on Confederation. He was among those who helped organize the administration of the new country and championed the right to education for the Protestant minority in Quebec. In 1866, he resigned from Cabinet when Upper Canada refused to offer the same right to the Catholic minority. However, when the final constitution was written, the right to education for religious minorities was in place.

He became Finance Minister in the Macdonald government and kept the office with a short break until Confederation. He was the first Finance Minister in the new Canadian government in 1867, but was forced to resign over the bankruptcy of the Commercial Bank of Kingston. He left politics for good in 1872, over his disagreement with a number of government policies. The remainder of his career was spent as Canada's representative abroad until he returned to business in 1883. During the 1880's, he formed a coal company to exploit the coal found near Lethbridge, Alberta. It was in this connection that he founded the town of Lethbridge. After 1890, he was forced to limit his activities due to illness. He died on September 19, 1893 at his home in Montreal.

The Fathers of Confederation   *Sir Alexander T. Galt*

Name: _____ **Date:** _____

Points to Ponder

1. Why did Galt come to Canada?
   _____
   _____

2. Why was his company beneficial to Canada?
   _____
   _____

3. Why did Galt favour annexation by the United States?
   _____
   _____

4. In what capacity did he serve as a delegate to the Confederation conferences?
   _____
   _____

5. How did his financial expertise benefit Canada?
   _____
   _____

🍁🍁 Explore History 🍁🍁

1. Make a list of the different currencies used throughout the world. How does the Canadian dollar compare with each one?

2. What was the reason the British American Land Company was formed?

3. Was there ever a chance that Canada would be annexed by the United States? Explain how this occurred.

4. Research Galt's connection to Lethbridge, Alberta. What did he do to be called the founder of the town?

© S&S Learning Materials

Fathers of Confederation

(Lt. Col.) John Hamilton Gray (1812 - 1887)
Prince Edward Island

There are two men named John Hamilton Gray among the Fathers of Confederation. This one was born in Prince Edward Island in 1812 and was educated in Charlottetown. He joined the British army at the age of nineteen and served as a cavalry officer in India and South Africa. He returned to Prince Edward Island in 1852 and entered politics in 1858 as the representative for Queen's County in the Island House of Assembly. He was re-elected in 1863 and served as the Premier until 1865.

As Premier of the host colony, he was the chairman of the Charlottetown Conference. Gray himself had little interest in Confederation and was embarrassed to be presiding over a conference that his voters did not support. Gray had not planned carefully for the delegates of the Charlottetown Conference. There were large crowds in Charlottetown who had come to see the circus and consequently, many of the delegates could not get hotel rooms. There was also no welcoming committee arranged for the arrival of the delegates.

When he heard the speeches and talked to the other delegates, he went on to the Conference in Quebec. However, his government was defeated in the general election which followed. The people of the Island had little interest in joining the other British North American colonies. There was little chance of an island town being chosen to be the capital of the new country; they would lose their Legislature and feared for their existence as a province. They also did not want to have any part of the railway debts which had been accumulated in other colonies.

Gray retired from politics and went back to military affairs as head of the militia. He died near Charlottetown on August 13, 1887.

Fathers of Confederation

John Hamilton Gray (1814 - 1889)
New Brunswick

The second John Hamilton Gray was born in St. George, Bermuda in 1814 where his father was based as a naval commissioner. He studied at King's College in Windsor, Nova Scotia where he earned a Bachelor's degree. He went on to study law and was admitted to the bar of New Brunswick in 1837. He established a practice in St. Ann where he quickly developed a reputation as a powerful courtroom speaker. He was made Queen's Counsel in 1853.

Gray began his political career in 1850 when he was elected to the Legislature as a Reformer. He became a leading member of the opposition, and so impressed the governor that he was invited to become a member of the Executive Council. This angered his colleagues in the Reform Party and was accused of wavering in his opinions. This reputation followed him for the rest of his political career. He became the Conservative leader in the Assembly, but became the leader of the Opposition once again in the election of 1854. Two years later, the Governor General dismissed the Assembly and replaced it with a government led by Gray.

Gray's term as Premier was short. By 1857, he was unable to maintain a majority in the House of Assembly and resigned. He tried to make a comeback in 1860 as a Liberal, but was defeated. While he was out of politics, he took part in several official inquiries such as the fishing dispute between Great Britain and the United States, the Absentee Landlords Question of Prince Edward Island and continued his law practice.

Gray was a staunch supporter of Confederation. He was chosen as a delegate to the Charlottetown and Quebec Conferences. He was not re-elected in the election which followed because he strongly supported Confederation, which was most unpopular at that time. Although he regained his seat in 1866, he was not invited to the London Conference.

He was elected to the first House of Commons in Ottawa, but did not run for re-election in 1872. That same year, he was appointed to the Supreme Court of British Columbia. There he was noted for his defence of the Chinese and for his authoritative work on the Canada - United States boundary disputes. In 1889, he was planning a reception for Tilley when he was stricken with paralysis. He died in June of that year.

Fathers of Confederation

Thomas Heath Haviland (1822 - 1895)

Thomas Heath Haviland was born in Charlottetown, Prince Edward Island on November 13, 1822. He grew up in a political atmosphere as his father had been in politics as long as Thomas could remember. Thomas was educated in Charlottetown and Brussels, Belgium. He studied law and was called to the bar in 1846.

In 1847, at the age of twenty-five, he became a member of the Legislative Assembly for Georgetown, and acted, in turn, as Colonial Secretary, Speaker of the House, and Solicitor General. In 1870, he was appointed to the Legislative Council and again acted as Colonial Secretary.

Thomas was not at the Charlottetown Conference, but he was a delegate at the Quebec Conference. He remained a supporter of Confederation even when it was rejected by the voters of Prince Edward Island. It was not until harder times came and the government debts were piling up, that the people changed their minds about Confederation. Haviland was one of three commissioners who negotiated the terms of union for Prince Edward Island to enter Confederation in 1873.

He was appointed to the Canadian Senate but resigned in 1879 to become Lieutenant Governor of Prince Edward Island. He died in Charlottetown on September 11, 1895.

The Fathers of Confederation   *Gray, Gray, and Haviland*

Name: _____ **Date:** _____

Points to Ponder

1. What mistakes did the older John Hamilton Gray make about the Charlottetown Conference?
   _____
   _____
   _____

2. Why didn't the people of Prince Edward Island want to join Confederation? What happened to change their minds?
   _____
   _____
   _____

3. What reputation did the younger John Hamilton Gray have? Why?
   _____
   _____

4. What work did the younger Gray do while on the Supreme Court of British Columbia?
   _____
   _____

5. What experience did Haviland have in politics?
   _____
   _____

🍁🍁 *Explore History* 🍁🍁

1. What impact did the British North American Land Company have on the settlement of Canada?

2. What was the Canada Company? Why did it fail?

3. What is the Supreme Court? How is it the same or different from the provincial court?

4. What was the position of Colonial Secretary?

Fathers of Confederation

William Alexander Henry (1816 - 1888)

William Alexander Henry was born on December 30, 1816 in Halifax, Nova Scotia. He was educated at Halifax High before going on to study law. He was admitted to the bar of Nova Scotia in 1840 and established a practice in Antigonish, and later Halifax. He was first elected to the Nova Scotia House of Representatives in 1840 as a Liberal, representing the largely Roman Catholic district of Antigonish even though Henry, himself, was a Protestant. This was accomplished with the help of the prominent Nova Scotian politician, Joseph Howe. In 1857, when Howe was Commissioner in charge of railway construction, Henry was defeated in the election due to Howe's denouncement of the Roman Catholic workers. At this time, Henry switched sides and turned his allegiance to the Conservative party.

In the Tupper government of 1863, Henry was appointed to the position of Attorney General and was a delegate to all three conferences on Confederation. Before the Charlottetown Conference, Henry showed little interest in the idea of union. His opinion changed dramatically at the first conference and he became convinced that Confederation would be the best way to achieve an Intercolonial Railway and free trade. He was not particularly active at the Quebec Conference, but he was part of the delegation that travelled to London. According to popular belief, it was Henry who adopted the Seventy-Two Resolutions to the British North America Act. However, he had objections to the limited number of senators and the division of federal and provincial powers. He was afraid that the will of the Senate would hamper the work of the House of Commons. He suggested that the government be given the authority to create new senators to override determined opposition. A clause was inserted in the British North America Act permitting the appointment of three or six additional senators on the recommendations of the Governor General. This, of course, weakened the independence for which the Senate was created. In spite of this, he voted to accept the agreement.

He ran for election for the seat of Antigonish in the federal general election and was defeated as Antigonish was one of the strongest anti-confederation ridings in the province. He returned to his law practice and in 1870 was elected as Mayor of Halifax. It was at this time that Henry again switched his allegiance back to the Liberal party. He was not satisfied with Sir John A. Macdonald's leadership and was resentful about being passed over for a judgeship in Nova Scotia. He was appointed to the newly formed Supreme Court of Canada in 1875. He attended all court proceedings and contributed to reforms to help the system run smoothly.

Fathers of Confederation

William Pearce Howland

John Mercer Johnson

Sir William Pearce Howland (1811 - 1907)

William Pearce Howland was born in Paulings, New York on May 29, 1811. He came to Upper Canada and set up a business in Cooksville in 1830. In 1840, he bought the Lambton Mills on the Humber River and later entered the wholesale groceries business in Toronto. He was interested in the reform movement, but kept away from the extreme views of William Lyon Mackenzie. He officially became a citizen of Canada in 1841.

In 1857, he was elected to the Legislative Assembly of the Province of Canada on a platform that promised to reform the government. He served in various ministries during the coalition government: Finance in 1862 and 1866; Receiver General in 1863; Postmaster General in 1864.

He was a delegate to the London Conference, having taken the place of Mowat who had been appointed to the bench in Canada West. He had a suggestion for curbing the blocking power of the Senate: the provinces would appoint the senators for a fixed term. However, he did not have support for this proposal. He was elected to the new government of Canada and was appointed to the position of Minister of Inland Revenue, but retired after the first session of Parliament.

From 1868 to 1873, he was Lieutenant Governor of Ontario. He then resumed his business interests in Toronto, where he died in 1907 at the age of ninety-six.

John Mercer Johnson (1818 - 1868)

John Mercer Johnson was born in Liverpool, England in October 1818. He came to New Brunswick as a boy and was educated at the Northumberland Grammar School. In 1840, he became a fully licenced lawyer. In 1850, he became the Liberal member in the legislature for Northumberland County and was one of the "Smashers" in the Cabinet of Charles Fisher. In the following years, he gained wide political experience serving in various portfolios such as Solicitor General, Postmaster General, Speaker of the House, and Attorney General. He was a delegate to all three conferences on Confederation.

He took exception to the amount of power which would be granted to the federal government, while giving his support to all other facets of the agreement. He lost his seat in 1865 over the Confederation issue, but was re-elected the following year. He was elected to the federal House of Commons in 1867, but his career in Ottawa was brief. He died on November 9, 1868.

© S&S Learning Materials

SSJ1-45

The Fathers of Confederation   *Henry, Howland, and Johnson*

Name: _____   **Date:** _____

Points to Ponder

1. Why did W. A. Henry decide to support Confederation?
   _____
   _____

2. What objections did Henry have to the Seventy-Two Resolutions?
   _____
   _____
   _____

3. How did Henry's objections affect the British North America Act?
   _____
   _____

4. What was Howland's suggestion for curbing the power of the Senate?
   _____
   _____

5. How did Johnson gain political experience?
   _____
   _____

🍁🍁 Explore History 🍁🍁

1. The clause that was inserted in the BNA Act concerning the appointment of Senators has changed. Research this clause and explain what that change is.

2. What are the duties of each of the following positions of government?

   a) Solicitor General
   b) Postmaster General
   c) Attorney General
   d) Speaker of the House

Fathers of Confederation

Sir Hector-Louis Langevin (1826 - 1906)

Hector Louis Langevin was born on August 25, 1826 in Quebec City, Lower Canada. He became a lawyer, studying for a time in the Montreal office of Sir George Étienne Cartier and was called to the bar of Lower Canada in 1850. However, it is for his careers in journalism and politics that he is best remembered. He began his career as a journalist in 1847, when he became editor of the weekly newspaper *Mélanges religieux*. He remained with the paper until 1849, but continued writing for other papers. He became editor of *Le Courrier du Canada* in 1857, the political editor of *Le Canadien* from 1872 - 1873 and the owner of *Le Monde* in 1884.

His political career went hand-in-hand with his journalistic career. He entered politics in 1856 when he was elected to the municipal council for Palais. Two years later, he became the Mayor of Quebec City and held that office until 1861. He was returned to the legislature in the 1857 - 1858 elections and later held the positions of Solicitor General from 1864 - 1866 and Postmaster General from 1866 - 1867.

While a member of the coalition government, he advocated a federation of the British North American colonies and took an active part in framing the constitution. He defended the interests of Quebec at all three conferences on Confederation. After Confederation, he was one of eighteen members who took seats in both the federal and provincial legislatures. He believed in the need for a strong federal government, but this opinion actually gave rise to provincial rights movements and the **Separatist movement** in Quebec.

Throughout the 1880's, he was Sir John A. Macdonald's right hand man in Quebec, but conflicts within the Conservative party undermined his influence. After the hanging of Louis Riel, Langevin was one of the few Conservatives to survive the 1887 election. He remained the Minister of Public Works. In 1891, he was charged with corruption in his department. He was found innocent of the corruption charges, but was found guilty of being negligent. He resigned from politics in 1896, after Prime Minister Abbott went back on his promise to make Langevin Lieutenant Governor of Quebec. He died in Quebec on June 11, 1906.

Andrew Archibald MacDonald (1829 - 1912)

Andrew Archibald MacDonald was born in Three Rivers, Prince Edward Island on February 14, 1829. He was educated at the local grammar school and through private tutoring after which he went into business as a merchant and shipowner. This was the era of the sailing ship and the fleets of the Maritime colonies ranked high in the world of commerce.

Fathers of Confederation

Andrew Archibald MacDonald

Jonathan McCully

He was elected to the Island Legislature in 1853 for a five year term. In 1863, he was elected to the Legislative Council and was appointed as a delegate to the Confederation Conferences. He was the youngest of the Fathers of Confederation at the age of thirty-five. Like the other Prince Edward Island delegates, he opposed the federal plan proposed by John A. Macdonald. He objected strongly to the number of seats in the Senate arguing for a larger representation of senators from the Maritime Provinces.

When Prince Edward Island did not join Confederation in 1867, MacDonald stayed on in the legislative council and became a member of the executive council or cabinet. When the Island joined Canada in 1873, he became Postmaster at Charlottetown. In 1884, he became Lieutenant Governor of Prince Edward Island. Later, he was appointed to the Canadian Senate where he served until his death in Ottawa on March 21, 1912.

Jonathan McCully (1809 - 1877)

Jonathan McCully was born in Cumberland County, Nova Scotia on July 25, 1809. He attended local schools and then went to work on a farm. He began teaching as soon as he finished school to save money to further his education. He studied law and after becoming a lawyer in 1837, opened a law office in Amherst, Nova Scotia.

McCully was a confirmed Liberal and expressed his view in frequent contributions to the *Acadian Recorder* and the *Morning Chronicle*. His support of Joseph Howe in the election of 1847 earned him an appointment to the Legislative Council. When the Liberals were re-elected in 1860, McCully was made Solicitor General as well as the sole railway commissioner. His policy of cutting cost rather than concentrating on efficiency and his lack of personal popularity caused Howe to blame him when the Liberals lost the election of 1863. His name was not on the first list of delegates to the Charlottetown Conference. When one of the other delegates withdrew at the last minute, Charles Tupper picked McCully as his replacement. Up until this time, McCully had not been a supporter of Confederation. His opinion of the proposal was changed by what he heard at the conference. Though he was not vocal at either Charlottetown, Quebec or London, he tried to promote the idea of Confederation by writing editorials in the local newspapers.

After Confederation became a reality, he was rewarded for his support by being appointed to the Senate. However, he was overshadowed by his more prominent colleagues. He was appointed as a judge in the Supreme Court of Nova Scotia in 1870. He died in Halifax on January 2, 1877.

The Fathers of Confederation   *Langevin, MacDonald, and McCully*

Name: _____ **Date:** _____

Points to Ponder

1. Why has it been said that Langevin began the Separatist movement?
   _____
   _____

2. Why is Langevin better known as a journalist than as a lawyer?
   _____
   _____

3. Why did A.A. MacDonald object to the number of seats in the Senate?
   _____
   _____

4. How did McCully hope to persuade the people of Nova Scotia to support Confederation?
   _____
   _____

5. Why was McCully blamed for the Liberal loss in the election of 1863?
   _____
   _____

🍁🍁 *Explore History* 🍁🍁

1. Who was Joseph Howe? What part did he play in the debate over Confederation?

2. What were the platforms on which the anti-confederates of Prince Edward Island and Nova Scotia convinced the voters to reject Confederation?

3. A.A. MacDonald wrote about the Charlottetown Conference. This was published in the March 1920 issue of the Canadian Historical Review. Try to find this issue and write a report about what he said.

Fathers of Confederation

William McDougall (1822 - 1905)

William McDougall was born on January 25, 1822 in Toronto, Upper Canada. He received his early education in Toronto and later in Cobourg. At the age of fifteen, he was a witness to the burning of **Montgomery's Tavern** by **Loyalists** in the Rebellion of 1837. In 1847, he started a career in law which actually enabled him to begin a career in journalism. He started in the field of agricultural journalism, but soon moved to publishing for the political newspaper *North American*. His work in politics began with his work in founding the Upper Canadian **Clear Grit** Reform Party. This party favoured political institutions, universal **suffrage** for everyone, free trade with the United States, the **secularization of the clergy** and representation by population. He supported the **Hincks-Monn coalition government** in exchange for the nomination of two Clear Grit representatives in the Cabinet. In 1858, he won his own seat and was a member of the Assembly of the Province of Canada from 1858 - 1867, serving as Commissioner of Lands from 1862 - 1864.

In 1867, he switched his political allegiance to the Conservative party. This earned him the nickname of **Wandering Willie**. He attended all three conferences on Confederation, causing quite a stir when he called for the election of the members of the Senate rather than appointment.

After Confederation, he was instrumental in purchasing **Rupert's Land** from the **Hudson's Bay Company**. He had always wanted to see Canada stretched to the West. He was appointed to the position of Lieutenant Governor of Rupert's Land in 1869, but came into conflict with Louis Riel. He was not actually a good candidate for the position because he wasn't trusted by the **Metis**. He was known to favour English speaking Protestant settlers which was what the Metis most feared. As well, McDougall could speak neither French nor the native languages, so he would not be able to communicate with those whom he had to govern. He returned to Ottawa in disgrace and opposed the entry of Manitoba into Confederation.

McDougall lived for many more years, remained in political life, but was never prominent again. He died on May 29, 1905.

The Fathers of Confederation   *William McDougall*

Name: _____ **Date:** _____

Points to Ponder

1. What were the aims of the Clear Grit Reform party?
   _____
   _____
   _____

2. What was McDougall's nickname? How did he get this name?
   _____
   _____

3. What did McDougall do at the Confederation conferences that caused a stir among the delegates?
   _____
   _____

4. How did McDougall achieve his dream of seeing Canada expand westward?
   _____
   _____

5. Why did he return to Ottawa from Rupert's land in disgrace?
   _____
   _____

6. Why was McDougall not a good candidate for the position of Lieutenant Governor of the Northwest Territories?
   _____
   _____

🍁🍁 Explore History 🍁🍁

1. How did Montgomery's Tavern play an important part in the Rebellion of 1837 - 1838?

2. What is suffrage? Why was it an issue in Canadian politics?

3. Who was Louis Riel? What part did he play in the history of Manitoba?

Fathers of Confederation

Thomas D'Arcy McGee (1825 - 1868)

Thomas D'Arcy McGee was born in Carlingford, Ireland on April 13, 1825. While he was still a child, his family moved to Wexford, Ireland where he received an informal education. In 1842, Thomas left Ireland and travelled to North America where he joined the staff of the *Boston Pilot*, a Catholic newspaper. Two years later, at the age of nineteen, he was the editor of the paper. He used this position to lobby for Irish independence and the rights of Irish Catholic immigrants. McGee also supported the American annexation of Canada. He returned to Ireland in 1845, but became involved in the Irish Rebellion of 1848 and was forced to flee to the United States. He continued to lobby for Irish independence, but when his projects failed to gain support, he moved to Montreal in 1857 at the invitation of the local Irish community.

By the time McGee came to Canada, his attitude toward the country had changed. He no longer supported annexation by the United States, and in fact, urged Irish immigrants to come to Canada rather than the United States. He also became editor of a Montreal newspaper, the *New Era* which he used to discuss Irish politics and the future of Canada. The work McGee did at the newspaper helped to launch his political career. In the pages of this newspaper, he called for the construction of a new nationality through the unification of British North America. He also lobbied for the construction of a railroad and for the creation of a province for Aboriginal Peoples.

In 1857, McGee was elected to the Legislative Assembly for the province of Canada as a member of George Brown's Reform government. Over the next several years, he tried to increase the support given to the Reform Party. He joined the Cabinet of John Sandfield MacDonald in 1862 and chaired the Intercolonial Conference in Quebec City. However, McGee was dropped from Cabinet when the railway plan fell through. Eventually, he broke with the Reformers and joined the Conservative party. In 1863, as part of the Conservative government, McGee became Minister of Agriculture, Immigration and Statistics. In 1864, he helped to organize the **Canadian Visit**, a diplomatic tour of the Maritimes that served as the prelude to Confederation. During this tour, McGee delivered many speeches in support of the Union and lived up to his reputation of being the most talented political **orator** of the era. He was chosen as a delegate to the Charlottetown and Quebec Conferences and in 1865, he delivered two speeches that were published. However, he was not invited to attend the London Conference and was not included in the Cabinet of the first Confederation government.

By 1868, McGee was planning to leave politics to spend more time on his writings. On April 7, 1868, he attended a late night sitting of the House of Commons. As he was returning home he was shot and killed. It is generally believed that his murder was arranged by the Fenian Movement of which he had been very critical.

The Fathers of Confederation   *Thomas D'Arcy McGee*

Name: _____   **Date:** _____

Points to Ponder

1. How did McGee show that he never forgot his Irish roots?
   _____
   _____
   _____

2. Once he moved to Canada, how did he show that he supported the growth of the country?
   _____
   _____
   _____

3. What was the Canadian Visit?
   _____
   _____
   _____

4. Why do you think McGee joined the Conservative party?
   _____
   _____
   _____

🍁🍁 Explore History 🍁🍁

1. Research the speeches of Thomas D'Arcy McGee. Summarize one of them for your class.

2. Create a poster that might have been distributed throughout the Maritimes to advertise the **Canadian Visit**.

3. Who were the **Fenians**? What part did they play in Canadian history?

4. Who was John Sandfield MacDonald?

Fathers of Confederation

Peter Mitchell (1824 - 1899)

Peter Mitchell was born in Newcastle, New Brunswick on January 24, 1824. He attended the local grammar school, studied law and set up a law practice there. He later left the profession of law and became engaged in two of New Brunswick's chief industries: lumbering and shipbuilding.

In 1850, he entered the Legislative Assembly as an independent member for Northumberland and in 1861, was appointed to the Legislative Council. For five years, he was a minister in the Fisher and Tupper administrations. He attended the Quebec Conference and strongly supported Confederation. He was defeated by the anti-Confederates in 1865, but was re-elected in 1866.

As a businessman, he was able to convince the St. John bankers of the advantages of Confederation. The bankers feared a loss of business to Canada. He also won the support of the fishermen and the shippers of the north shore by insisting that the Intercolonial Railway should follow the Gulf of St. Lawrence and not take an inland route. He was asked to form a government with R. D. Wilmot as joint Premier. It was in this capacity as Premier of New Brunswick, that Mitchell went to London to negotiate the terms of union for his province's entry into Confederation.

In 1867, he was appointed to the Canadian Senate and acted as Minister of Marine and Fisheries for five years. His independence led him to resign his office and to seek a seat in the House of Commons. His political career was always highlighted by his stubbornness. An example of this stubbornness could be seen when he delayed the approval of the estimates for the Intercolonial Railway until a widow received compensation for a cow that had been killed by a train. He also had a long-standing feud with Sir Leonard Tilley, another Father of Confederation.

He became the editor and later the owner of the *Montreal Herald*. The last three years of his life were spent as an inspector of fisheries for the Maritime Provinces. He died on October 25, 1899.

Fathers of Confederation

Sir Oliver Mowat (1820 - 1903)

Oliver Mowat was born in Kingston on July 22, 1820. He inherited firmly-held religious convictions from his Scottish Presbyterian parents and considered Christian statesmanship his vocation. He attended private schools and studied law, becoming a lawyer in 1841. He was Sir John A. Macdonald's first articled law student.

In spite of his relationship with Macdonald, Mowat entered politics as a Liberal member for Ontario South in the assembly of the Province of Canada serving first as Provincial Secretary and then as Postmaster General. He was secretary in the Brown-Dorian Coalition (which only lasted two days). He reluctantly entered the coalition government of Macdonald and Cartier and only after the promise that the constitutional issue would be settled.

As a Cabinet Minister, he was a delegate to the Quebec Conference where he was responsible for the resolution concerning the legislative power of the provincial governments. He resigned soon after the conference to become vice-chancellor of Upper Canada. He became Premier of Ontario when Edward Blake resigned in 1872. He kept this position for the next twenty-four years. Also acting as Attorney General, he introduced the practice of voting by ballot in provincial and municipal elections and also allowed more people to have the right to vote.

Even though Mowat was not a chief architect of Confederation, he did much to determine the form that Confederation took in its first forty years. As Premier of Ontario, he had many battles with the federal government for provincial rights. He was responsible for the power acquired by legislatures to act as fully responsible bodies in matters of provincial concern.

When Sir Wilfrid Laurier came to power in 1896, Mowat was appointed to the Senate as government leader and Minister of Justice. However at the age of seventy-seven, he found the work too demanding and so retired from political life. He was named Lieutenant Governor of Ontario in 1897. He died in Toronto on April 19, 1903.

The Fathers of Confederation   *Mitchell and Mowat*

Name: _____ **Date:** _____

Points to Ponder

1. How was Mitchell's experience in business helpful in his campaign for Confederation?
   _____
   _____

2. How did Mitchell win the support of the fishermen?
   _____
   _____

3. How did Mitchell demonstrate that he was a very stubborn person?
   _____
   _____

4. What rights do we enjoy today in an election as the result of the efforts of Sir Oliver Mowat?
   _____
   _____

5. How did Mowat help form the relationship between the provinces and the federal government?
   _____
   _____

🍁🍁 Explore History 🍁🍁

1. Research the areas that lie within the jurisdiction of the federal and provincial governments. Make a list of the responsibilities of each government.

2. When were women allowed to vote in Canada? Did it differ in each province? Make a timeline of the women's suffrage in Canada.

3. What events led to the Brown-Dorian coalition government? Why did it last only two days?

© S&S Learning Materials

Fathers of Confederation

Edward Palmer (1809 - 1889)

Edward Palmer was born on September 1, 1809 in Charlottetown, Prince Edward Island. He attended grammar school before studying law at his father's office and was called to the bar in 1830. He worked as a lawyer, land agent, landed proprietor, politician and judge. He became a member of the Prince Edward Island legislature in 1835, quickly establishing himself as a leading Conservative. He was often viewed as a champion of the **status quo**: he was against responsible government, against union with British North America, and was part of a major land owning family against land reform. He eventually sold his land in 1870 after experiencing difficulties with his tenants. He also was involved in many conflicts in the Assembly, frequently arguing with Coles and Whelan. In 1849, he became leader of the Conservative party and in 1859, he became Premier of Prince Edward Island.

Palmer was a delegate at both the Charlottetown and Quebec conferences, where he demonstrated his strong opposition to Confederation. He called himself "the malcontent of the conference". He did not agree with the terms of union being offered to Prince Edward Island. This caused a rift in the Conservative party and damaged the cause of Confederation resulting in Palmer resigning from Cabinet. He did, however, keep his position as Attorney General.

After the two conferences, Palmer remained opposed to Confederation. He opposed the **Better Terms** offer by the Canadian government in 1869 and instead favoured a trade deal between the Island and the United States. In 1872, he changed parties and joined the Liberal, anti-Confederation party of Robert Haythorne. When the debts of the railway pushed Prince Edward Island to the brink of economic collapse in 1873, it was actually Haythorne who approached the Canadian government regarding the Island's entry into Confederation. Palmer had changed his mind by this time and went to London with W.H. Pope to negotiate the terms for entry into the union.

After Confederation, Palmer became a Queens County judge. He later became Chief Justice of the same court, a position he held until his death in Charlottetown on November 3, 1889. In his lifetime, he had spent thirty-eight years in parliamentary work.

The Fathers of Confederation   *Edward Palmer*

Name: _____ **Date:** _____

Points to Ponder

1. What does it mean to say that Palmer was a supporter of the status quo?
   _____
   _____
   _____

2. Why did he oppose Confederation?
   _____
   _____
   _____

3. Why did Palmer switch his allegiance from the Conservative party to the Liberals?
   _____
   _____
   _____

4. What changed his mind about supporting Confederation?
   _____
   _____
   _____

🍁🍁 Explore History 🍁🍁

1. What problems arose in Prince Edward Island in the 1870's that forced it to consider joining Canada?

2. What were the terms of Union by which Prince Edward Island joined Confederation?

3. How were these terms different from what had been offered in 1867?

Fathers of Confederation

William Henry Pope (1825 - 1879)

William Henry Pope was born on May 29, 1825 in Bedeque, Prince Edward Island. He was educated on the Island, and later in England before studying law under Edward Palmer. He was called to the bar in 1847. In addition to being a lawyer, Pope was also a land agent. Through his family's prominent connections, he was able to obtain many influential clients.

During the 1850's, Pope became involved with the Conservative party. In 1859, he was appointed to the position of Colonial Secretary under the government's new policy of **nondepartmentalism** which was an effort to combat **patronage**. The government was trying an experiment of having civil servants head the government departments. He also became editor of the Island's Conservative newspaper *The Islander*. The main issue facing the government at this time was that of Absentee Landlords. Pope believed that property rights had to be respected and that the Imperial government was to blame for the problems.

He also became involved in attempts to reconcile the differences which existed between the Protestants and Catholics of Prince Edward Island that arose during the 1859 elections. After several failed attempts, it was decided that the Conservative party would be largely supported by the Protestants, which resulted in a Conservative win in the 1863 election. Pope entered the Legislature as the member for Belfast and kept his post as Colonial Secretary. Early in his term, he was appointed as a member of a three-person commission to study the lands question, and to make recommendations to the Imperial government.

Pope was one of a few politicians from Prince Edward Island who supported Confederation. He attended both the Charlottetown and Quebec Conferences acting as Honorary Secretary in Quebec. This put him at odds with Edward Palmer and the resulting confusion prevented the Conservatives from forming the next government. His brother, James, formed an interim government, but William became increasingly isolated from the other members of the Legislature. In 1866, when James passed a "No Terms" resolution against Confederation, William was away on a trade mission. He resigned his seat over this matter and did not run in the 1867 election.

He continued to support Confederation through letters and lectures as well as rebuilding the Conservative party into a pro-Confederation party. He won a seat in the government in 1873, on a campaign promise to obtain better terms of union for Prince Edward Island. He was appointed to the position of Prince County Court Judge after Confederation and was extremely successful. In 1878, he did a revision of the province's statutes and was preparing a history of Prince Edward Island at the time of his death in Summerside on October 7, 1879.

The Fathers of Confederation *William Henry Pope*

Name: _____ **Date:** _____

Points to Ponder

1. How did Pope gain a government position without being elected?
   _____
   _____
   _____
   _____

2. How did Pope feel about the issue of Absentee Landlords?
   _____
   _____
   _____
   _____

3. How did Pope differ from his fellow Conservatives about Confederation?
   _____
   _____
   _____
   _____

4. How did he continue to support Confederation?
   _____
   _____
   _____
   _____

🍁🍁 *Explore History* 🍁🍁

1. Who was James Pope? How long was he Premier of Prince Edward Island? Write a report on him for your class.

2. Create a poster that might have been used to try to convince Prince Edward Island voters of the benefits of Confederation.

3. Do you think Prince Edward Island should have joined Confederation in 1867? Why or why not?

Fathers of Confederation

John William Ritchie

Sir Ambrose Shea

John William Ritchie (1808 - 1890)

John William Ritchie was born in Annapolis, Nova Scotia, on March 26, 1808. He was raised in a legal atmosphere as his father was the county judge. He was educated privately and became a qualified lawyer in 1833. His first public office was as a clerk to the Legislative Council in Halifax. He later became a member of the Council and became part of the Cabinet as Solicitor General.

He maintained his support of Confederation, especially concerning the commercial advantages that such a union would give Nova Scotia. He felt that all the colonies should be concerned with the renewal of the Reciprocity Treaty and not just leave it to the Province of Canada. He was part of the **Confederate Council on Commercial Treaties** which met in Quebec in 1865 to study the question of colonial trade. This council suggested that the provinces take joint action in commercial policies, that trade missions be sent to the West Indies and South America and that one of its members be invited to act with the British minister at the negotiations in Washington. It was partly because of his work on this committee that he was invited to be a delegate at the final conference on Confederation in London.

In 1867, he was appointed to the Senate and three years later to the Supreme Court of Nova Scotia. In 1873, he was made a judge in equity and served in this office for the next nine years. Ritchie died in Halifax on December 28, 1890.

Sir Ambrose Shea (1815 - 1905)

Ambrose Shea was born in St. John's, Newfoundland on September 17, 1815. He was educated in St. John's and worked for a time on *The Newfoundlander* a family-owned newspaper, before going into business on his own. By the 1850's, he was a successful merchant dealing in insurance and the transatlantic steamer trade. He continued to operate this business even while he was in politics.

In 1848, he ran in an election and won a seat as a Liberal representing Placentia - St. Mary's. He was a supporter of responsible government and was a spokesman for reciprocity with the United States acting as the delegate to Washington in 1853. In the first responsible government election of 1855, Shea was returned to the Legislature as the member for St. John's West and was appointed to the position of Speaker of the House.

Fathers of Confederation

John William Ritchie

Sir Ambrose Shea

Shea was asked to be one of two delegates to the Quebec Conference. He was an enthusiastic supporter of the Seventy-Two Resolutions giving a speech in their favour at a dinner in Montreal. He was especially concerned with the poverty of Newfoundlanders and he hoped that by joining Confederation the colony would gain financially. However, his attendance at the conference was as an observer only. He had not taken into consideration that Confederation was a new idea, and had not really been widely discussed at home. The merchants also intimidated the fishing class, warning them of increased taxes, higher prices, and other dreadful economic results if they voted for Confederation. Therefore, upon his return to Newfoundland he found that the majority of the voters were not in favour of Confederation. He was unable to sway even the Catholic opinion in his favour. His plan to promote union by employing Newfoundlanders on the Intercolonial Railway was unsuccessful, as many men either failed to find work or drifted away without returning to the Island. In 1869, he campaigned against Charles Bennett's anti-Confederate campaign and was defeated.

Following this defeat, Shea stayed out of public life for a while. In 1873, he ran again for election, but was defeated in St. John's East. He was elected in Harbour Grace in January. Under the administration of F.B.T. Carter, he had considerable influence in the Executive Council. He was one of the primary supporters of railway construction and a member of the joint committee that recommended establishment of a railway line in 1880.

Many people felt that Shea was an embarrassment to the Newfoundland government He was appointed as Governor of the Bahamas and served there from 1887 to 1894. He maintained an interest in Newfoundland affairs and attempted to participate in the 1888 Confederation negotiations. When his term as Governor ended, he retired to London, where he died in 1905.

The Fathers of Confederation *Ritchie and Shea*

Name: _____ **Date:** _____

Points to Ponder

1. What was the Confederate Council on Commercial Treaties? What was its recommendation?
   _____
   _____

2. Why was Shea so supportive of the Seventy-Two Resolutions?
   _____
   _____

3. How did the Newfoundland merchants persuade people to vote against Confederation?
   _____
   _____
   _____

4. How did Shea plan to use the Intercolonial Railway to promote Confederation? What was the result?
   _____
   _____

5. Why do you think Shea was regarded as an embarrassment?
   _____
   _____

🍁🍁 *Explore History* 🍁🍁

1. What was the relationship that existed between the merchants and the fishermen in Newfoundland? Why was it beneficial for the merchants that Newfoundland did not join the Confederation?

2. What were the main trade goods of each of the following colonies:
   a) Newfoundland
   b) Nova Scotia
   c) New Brunswick
   d) Prince Edward Island
   e) Canada East
   f) Canada West

Fathers of Confederation

William Henry Steeves (1814 - 1873)

William Henry Steeves was born in Hillsborough on the Petitcodiac River in New Brunswick on May 20, 1814. His family were lumbermen and shipbuilders, and William grew up in this business. In 1846, he became a Liberal member in the Legislative Assembly for Albert County and held this seat for five years. He was then appointed to the Legislative Council and was named to the Executive Council first as surveyor general for a year and then as Minister of Public Works for eight years.

Railways were very much in the minds of the people of New Brunswick and Steeves was one of several men who were interested in building an intercolonial railroad. He went, with other members, to Quebec to discuss the matter of the railroad as well as free trade among the provinces. It was probably because of his business background and his business approach to matters, that he was chosen as one of New Brunswick's delegates to the Charlottetown and Quebec conferences.

He did not take an active part in the proceedings at the conferences, but he did give strong support to the idea of Confederation. He did not lose his seat in the next election as did the other delegates.

After Confederation, Steeves was chosen as a representative of New Brunswick in the Senate. He died in St. John, New Brunswick on December 9, 1873.

Fathers of Confederation

Sir Étienne-Paschal Tache (1795 - 1865)

Étienne-Paschal was born in St. Thomas de Montmagny, Quebec on September 5, 1795. He was educated at the seminary in Quebec and while still a teenager, he enlisted in the militia and fought in the War of 1812. After the war, he studied medicine and set up his doctor's office in his hometown. There he was regarded as a dignified country gentleman. He did not take part in the Rebellions of 1837 - 1838, but he did attend conferences and organize meetings. He was called a patriot who became a man of compromise when the **Act of Union** was adopted in 1841.

He entered political life with the first elections under the Union and was elected the member for the riding of L'Islet. From 1841 - 1846, he remained in the background of the major political debates and spoke very little in the House of Assembly. However, when he did give a speech in 1846 on the need to establish a militia for Lower Canada, his colleagues in the House took notice. Two months after this speech, he was named Deputy Adjutant-General of the militia in the **Draper - Papineau government**. In this position, he was responsible for reorganizing the armed forces of Lower Canada. In 1848, he was appointed to the Executive Council and named Chief Commissioner of Public Works in the **LaFontaine - Baldwin government**. From 1848 to 1857, he participated in every government. In 1837 and 1838, he had been considered a **Patriot**, but in the late 1850's he fought against the radicalism of the **Parti Rouge**.

In 1855 - 1856, Tache formed a government with Allan Napier MacNab. Under this government, he was Prime Minister of Lower Canada. When MacNab was forced to resign, Tache chose John A. Macdonald to form a new government until 1857. This was the first sign of an **alliance** between the Liberals in Lower Canada and Conservatives in Upper Canada.

Tache left active involvement in political life after the elections of 1857. He founded the newspaper *Le Courier du Canada* with Hector-Louis Langevin. It was in this paper that Tache presented his vision of confederation, a topic growing in popularity within the intellectual and political circles of both Upper and Lower Canada. He returned to political life after being invited by Governor Monck to form another government with John A. MacDonald. This government lasted only a month, a sure sign that the government of the United Canadas was not working. He resigned again because of ill-health.

In 1864, Tache was called out of retirement to help create the Great Coalition. This was mainly because he was known as a man who was impartial. He remained a member of the government and although he agreed with the principles of Confederation, he was not aware of the negative effect it might have on Lower Canada. He was the chairman for the Quebec Conference and was responsible for promoting the Seventy-Two Resolutions to the Legislative Council. He did not get to serve as a member of the Confederation government. He died on July 30, 1865.

The Fathers of Confederation   *Steeves and Tache*

Name: _____ **Date:** _____

Points to Ponder

1. Why do you think that William Henry Steeves was chosen as a delegate to the Confederation Conferences?
   _____
   _____

2. Why do you think Étienne Tache was such a help to John A. Macdonald in promoting Confederation?
   _____
   _____

3. Why was Tache called out of retirement to help form a new government in 1864?
   _____
   _____

4. What made Tache's colleagues in the House of Assembly sit up and take notice of him?
   _____

5. Why do you think that Tache made a good choice for the head of the militia?
   _____
   _____

🍁🍁 *Explore History* 🍁🍁

1. Research each of the following coalition governments and tell the main points of each:
        a) Draper - Papineau
        b) LaFontaine - Baldwin
        c) Macdonald - Tache

2. Tache was once called a **Patriot**. What is the significance of this name?

3. What was the Parti Rouge?

Fathers of Confederation

Sir Samuel Leonard Tilley (1818 - 1896)

Sameul Tilley was born in Gagetown, New Brunswick on May 8, 1818. He studied at the Church of England Madras School and then at a grammar school before becoming an apprentice druggist in Saint John in 1831. He became a certified pharmacist in 1838 and opened his own drugstore with a business partner. He took over the business himself when his partner retired. He later sold this business in the 1860's when he became involved in politics.

Tilley's political life was closely linked with his religious beliefs. He was a Sunday school teacher and believed in temperance and prohibition. He was part of the political group known as the "Smashers" which was unsuccessful in introducing prohibition to New Brunswick. He was a strong supporter of both responsible government and the Intercolonial Railway. He was first elected to the New Brunswick Legislature in 1850 as a representative of Saint John. He was a member of the Legislature almost continuously from 1850 to 1867, holding the position of Premier from 1861 to 1865 and again from 1866 to 1867.

Tilley was a strong supporter of Confederation and was a delegate to all three conferences. He supported the Seventy-Two Resolutions passed at Quebec even though they were unpopular among the New Brunswick voters. It was his support of Confederation that caused him to lose the election of 1865 to Albert Smith, an anti-Confederate. After this government failed, Tilley was returned to power and in 1866, he passed a resolution in the Assembly which supported Confederation. At the London Conference, it was Tilley who suggested the word "Dominion" as the title of the new nation of Canada after reading from Psalm 72 "He shall have Dominion from sea to sea and from the river unto the ends of the earth".

He was given the portfolio of Customs in the first federal Cabinet and became Lieutenant Governor of New Brunswick when the Macdonald government fell after the Pacific Scandal. However, he returned to the Cabinet in 1878 as Minister of Finance. He was instrumental in drawing up the **National Policy** during his second term. In 1885, he retired from the government and returned to his post as Lieutenant Governor in which post he served until 1893. After his retirement, he continued to take an active interest in politics at both the provincial and federal levels until his death on June 25, 1896. As he lay dying, his party was winning in New Brunswick while being defeated in the rest of Canada. His last words were, "I can go to sleep now. New Brunswick has done well."

Fathers of Confederation

Sir Charles Tupper (1821 - 1915)

Charles Tupper was born in Amherst, Nova Scotia on July 2, 1821. He studied at Horton Academy (now Acadia University) before going on to study medicine at the University of Scotland in Edinburgh. He became a doctor in 1843 and set up a medical practice in Amherst. He also set up another practice in Halifax in 1859 and served the city and provincial hospitals. He was President of the Medical Society of Nova Scotia in 1863 and was the first president of the Canadian Medical Association from 1867 to 1870. Throughout his political career, he continued to be a doctor at heart, setting up practices in Toronto and Ottawa and was rumoured to have kept his medical bag under his seat in the House of Commons.

Tupper entered politics by winning a seat for the Conservatives in Cumberland County, Nova Scotia when he defeated the well-known Joseph Howe. He worked hard to improve the party and eventually took over as leader. In 1857, the Liberal government was defeated and Tupper became provincial secretary until 1860. In this office, he opened negotiations with the Province of Canada and New Brunswick to build an Intercolonial Railway. After a brief period in opposition, the Conservatives were returned to power in 1863. Tupper served another term as provincial secretary and then became Premier on May 11, 1864.

Tupper was instrumental in developing the impetus behind the push for Confederation. He arranged the Charlottetown Conference to discuss the possibility of forming a union of the Maritime colonies of Nova Scotia, New Brunswick, Prince Edward Island and Newfoundland. He agreed to welcome the delegates from the Province of Canada and then changed his mind to push for Confederation of all of British North America. He was a strong supporter of Confederation believing that Nova Scotia would greatly benefit from such a union. He headed the delegations to Charlottetown and Quebec, and did not believe there would be any problems passing the Seventy-Two Resolutions in the Nova Scotia Legislature. When he did meet with opposition, he was able to stall taking a vote until the last possible minute. He assured the people that he would be able to secure better terms of union for the province during the London Conference.

When Confederation became a reality, Tupper entered federal politics, but did not receive a Cabinet post because of regional representation concerns. He also refused a position with the Intercolonial Railway Commission because he wanted to maintain his influence and credibility in Nova Scotia. In 1868, he went to London to try to counteract Joseph Howe and his attempt to withdraw Nova Scotia from Confederation. He succeeded in winning Howe over to the side of Confederation.

Fathers of Confederation

Tupper held a number of Cabinet posts until the collapse of the government in 1873. While he was not implicated in the Pacific Scandal, he defended those who were and was one of the strongest opposition voices in the House of Commons. When the Conservatives returned to power in 1878, Tupper became Minister of Public Works. This ministry was split in 1879, with Tupper taking over the area of railways and canals. It was during this term that Tupper oversaw the completion of the **Canadian Pacific Railway**, the expansion of the **Welland Canal** and advocated expansion of many local railway lines.

The controversy over the Canadian Pacific Railway strained the relationship between Tupper and John A. Macdonald so Tupper decided to accept an appointment as High Commissioner to London in 1884. He returned to Canada at Macdonald's request for the 1886 election, in part to combat the resurgence of **secessionism** in Nova Scotia by **William Fielding**. When the Conservatives won the election, he became Minister of Finance in 1887.

In 1888, Tupper returned to his position as High Commissioner. He was a forceful advocate for Canada promoting emigration to Canada from all over the British Isles, as well as the agricultural and commercial interests of the country. He gained an increasing power at the highest levels of British society, taking an active role in international negotiations on behalf of both countries.

His prominence in the Conservative party led many to think that he would be Prime Minister following the death of Sir John A. Macdonald, but it was not until 1896, when the Manitoba Schools Question forced the resignation of Mackenzie Bowells that Tupper gained the position. Tupper was forced to dissolve the House after only ten weeks over the Schools Question. His was the shortest term as Prime Minister in the history of Canada. In the election which followed, the Conservative party was defeated. Tupper worked hard to try to rebuild the Conservative party. While in opposition, he even tried to use the **Boer War** to undermine the Liberal government. When the party was again defeated in 1900, Tupper resigned as leader.

His remaining years were spent at Bexleyheath, England at the home of his married daughter although he made frequent trips to Canada to visit his sons. He was appointed to the British Privy Council in 1907 and also served on the committee of the British Empire League. He died in England on October 30, 1915; the longest surviving Father of Confederation.

The Fathers of Confederation   *Tilley and Tupper*

Name: _____ **Date:** _____

Points to Ponder

1. How did Sir Leonard Tilley choose the name for Canada?
   _____
   _____

2. How was this psalm fitting for the new nation of Canada?
   _____
   _____

3. How did Sir Charles Tupper actually initiate Confederation?
   _____
   _____

4. What did Tupper achieve while in the federal Cabinet?
   _____
   _____

5. Why did he return from London in 1886?
   _____
   _____

🍁🍁 Explore History 🍁🍁

1. What was the National Policy that Tilley drafted?

2. What was the **Boer War**? What part did Canada play in this war?

3. What was **secessionism** in Nova Scotia? Who was **William Fielding**?

4. What does the position of High Commissioner to London involve? Is it still an active position?

Fathers of Confederation

Edward Whelan (1824 - 1867)

Edward Whelan was born in Ballina, County Mayo, Ireland in 1824. The exact date of his birth and very little about his early life in known. He received a basic education in Ballina and also in Scotland. He and his mother emigrated to Halifax in 1831. There, he enrolled in St. Mary's School and apprenticed in the printing office of Joseph Howe who had a major influence on him. Howe encouraged him to read widely and to practise public speaking. At the age of eighteen, he left Howe's shop to become editor of the Irish Catholic newspaper, *The Register*. He made a name for himself as a talented speaker. In 1843, he moved to Charlottetown, where he founded his own paper, *The Palladium* and developed a reputation as an outspoken, reform-minded journalist.

His political career began in 1846, when he was elected to the Assembly of Prince Edward Island as a member for St. Peters. Both in the Assembly and through the pages of *The Palladium*, he agitated for reform of the absentee landlord system and the political system of the Island. He received wide support in every way but financially. He went bankrupt and was forced to accept the editorship of his hated rival, *The Morning News*. In 1847, he established another newspaper, *The Examiner*. He used this paper to fight for responsible government. He was so outspoken that he was frequently sued for libel. When responsible government was attained in 1851, Whelan was made a member of the Executive Council. He became Queen's Printer until 1859 at which time he temporarily suspended his own paper to begin production of *The Royal Gazette*. He was a strong defender of the Liberal policies on land reform and education until the defeat of the party in 1859.

When discussion on possible Confederation developed in the 1860's, Whelan was the only Liberal not opposed to the idea. He was a delegate to the Charlottetown Conference where he declared that his support was a way to free the island from control of the Colonial Office and a way to solve the problem of absentee landlords. He was also a delegate to Quebec and he promoted Confederation through *The Examiner*. He found very little support for his ideas in Prince Edward Island and his support of the Tenant League cost him the votes of the Irish Catholics.

When the Liberals regained power in 1867, Whelan was once again named Queen's Printer. This position required him to resign his seat and run again. He did so, but was defeated. and blamed his loss on the local clergy. His health began to deteriorate after this and he died on December 10, 1867.

Fathers of Confederation

Robert Duncan Wilmot (1809 - 1891)

Robert Duncan Wilmot was born in Fredericton on October 16, 1809. He was educated in Saint John and went into the lumbering and shipping business. In 1840, he became interested in Liberal ideas and was elected to the New Brunswick Legislature in 1846. He was not, however, a confirmed Liberal and accepted office in the Conservative Cabinet as Surveyor General in 1851, and as Provincial Secretary in 1856.

After studying the Seventy-Two Resolutions, he became an anti-Confederate. He believed that it gave too much power to the central government. Along with Albert Smith, he headed the anti-Confederate government after the overthrow of the Tilley administration in 1865. However, this proved to be a very contentious and ineffective administration. Wilmot was also a member of the Confederate Council on Commercial Treaties. It was while attending a meeting of this council that he realized Canada East would never accept legislative union. If there was to be Confederation, it would have to be a federal union such as was planned at Quebec. He therefore became a supporter of Confederation.

He resigned from the Smith-Wilmot administration in March 1866 and formed a Confederate government with Mitchell when Smith resigned a month later. He was also a delegate to the London Conference. In the new Canadian government, Wilmot was given a seat in the Senate. In 1878, he became Speaker of the Senate and a minister without portfolio in Macdonald's reconstructed administration.

In 1880, he resigned his seat in the Senate to become the Lieutenant Governor of New Brunswick. He died on February 12, 1891.

The Fathers of Confederation   *Whelan and Wilmot*

Name: _____   **Date:** _____

Points to Ponder

1. What did Edward Whelan use his newspaper for?
   _____
   _____
   _____

2. Why did Whelan go bankrupt when many people supported his ideas?
   _____
   _____

3. Why did he support Confederation?
   _____
   _____

4. Why did Wilmot become an anti-Confederate?
   _____
   _____

5. How was his mind changed about Confederation?
   _____
   _____

🍁 🍁 Explore History 🍁 🍁

1. How have newspapers been used throughout the years to further political causes? Give examples.

2. What were the claims of those opposed to Confederation in the British North American colonies?

3. What is bankruptcy? How does one apply for bankruptcy? What are the effects of bankruptcy?

© S&S Learning Materials

Fathers of Confederation

Who Were They?

Who were the Fathers of Confederation?

Make a list of all the delegates you have read about and complete the following table.

Name	Province Represented	Occupation

The Fathers of Confederation — Who Were They?

Name	Province Represented	Occupation

The Fathers of Confederation   *Who Were They?*

Name	Province Represented	Occupation

The Fathers of Confederation   *Who Were They?*

Name	Province Represented	Occupation

The Fathers of Confederation

Quiz 1

Name: _____ Date: _____

Answer each of the following questions in full sentences:

1. What does the term "Fathers of Confederation" mean?
   _____
   _____
   _____
   _____

2. Where did the name "Dominion of Canada" come from?
   _____
   _____
   _____
   _____

3. Where were the three conferences on Confederation held?
   _____
   _____
   _____
   _____

4. What provinces joined Confederation in 1867?
   _____
   _____
   _____
   _____

5. What was the British North America Act?
   _____
   _____
   _____
   _____

The Fathers of Confederation   Quiz 1

6. What were the Seventy-Two Resolutions? Why are they sometimes called the "Quebec Resolutions"?

   _____
   _____
   _____
   _____

7. Why didn't the Maritime provinces support Confederation at first?

   _____
   _____
   _____
   _____

8. What were some factors which led politicians to try to achieve Confederation?

   _____
   _____
   _____
   _____

9. What was "representation by population"? Who came up with this phrase?

   _____
   _____
   _____
   _____

10. What part did John A. Macdonald play in the Charlottetown and Quebec Conferences?

    _____
    _____
    _____
    _____

The Fathers of Confederation

Quiz 2

Name: _____   Date: _____

Part A

Match each of the following Fathers of Confederation with an event with which he was directly involved.

1. Sir John A. Macdonald _____
2. Sir Charles Tupper _____
3. Edward Whelan _____
4. Sir Alexander Galt _____
5. Sir Étienne-Paschal Tache _____
6. Sir Georges-Étienne Cartier _____
7. William McDougall _____
8. Thomas D'Arcy McGee _____
9. Leonard Tilley _____
10. Jean-Charles Chapais _____

a) Battle of St. Denis
b) purchase of Rupert's Land
c) organized the Canadian Visit
d) drafted the National Policy
e) gave the first Order in Council
f) supported annexation by the U.S.
g) was the only Liberal to support Confederation
h) was High Commissioner to London
i) was the father of Canada
j) was the first to form an alliance with John A. Macdonald

Part B

Give the nickname of each of the following:

1. Sir John A. Macdonald _____
2. John Mercer Johnson _____
3. Jean-Charles Chapais _____
4. Frederic Carter _____
5. William McDougall _____

© S&S Learning Materials　　　　　　　　　　SSJ1-45

The Fathers of Confederation Quiz 2

Part C

Write short notes on each of the following:

1. The Placeman's Bill

2. Smashers and Rummies

3. representation by population

4. The Canadian Visit

5. The Charlottetown Conference

The Fathers of Confederation Quiz 2

Tell whether the following statements are True or False:

1. John A. Macdonald did not originally support Confederation. _____

2. George Brown was from Canada East. _____

3. Sir Charles Tupper was a representative from Newfoundland. _____

4. William McDougall was not allowed to enter the Northwest Territories. _____

5. Robert Duncan Wilmot was Minister of Finance in the Macdonald government. _____

6. Thomas D'Arcy McGee was famous for his speeches. _____

7. Edward Whelan was an Irish catholic. _____

8. Sir Oliver Mowat helped make most of the changes to federal-provincial regulations. _____

9. Sir Samuel Leonard Tilley came up with the idea of using dollars and cents for Canadian money. _____

10. Wiliam Henry Pope argued with his brother over Confederation. _____

11. Sir Alexander Galt came up with the name for Canada. _____

12. Edward Palmer helped bring Prince Edward Island into Confederation. _____

13. Frederic Carter was regarded as an embarrassment to Newfoundland. _____

14. Sir Étienne-Paschal Tache spoke French. _____

15. Peter Mitchell was extremely stubborn. _____

The Fathers of Confederation
Answer Key

Introduction: *(page 10)*
1. The forces which led to the meeting in Charlottetown were:
   a) the possibility of annexation by the United States
   b) the deadlock in which the politicians of the Province of Canada found themselves
   c) the need to unite to get better trade agreements.
   d) The politicians of the Province of Canada wanted to join the meeting because they had been talking about this sort of thing and the Maritimers had come up with the idea of a meeting.
2. The result of the Quebec Conference was the drawing up of the Seventy-Two resolutions which formed the basis of the government of the new nation.
3. They were delighted with the idea because they were finding the cost of defending the colonies too high.
4. The result of the London Conference was the signing of the British North America Act which made Canada a new nation.
5. It refers to the men who were present at all three Confederation conferences.

Sir John A. Macdonald: *(page 13)*
1. He took over the practice of a sick relative and then opened his own office.
2. He chose instead to try to broaden the party base.
3. He formed a coalition with George Brown because he knew that cooperating with the politicians from Canada West was the only way the government would be able to get any work done.
4. He knew that Tache would be better at dealing with the French speaking voters.
5. He agreed to Confederation to try to restore some order to the government.

George Brown: *(page 15)*
1. He used the paper as a way of preaching his ideas on settling and colonizing the West.
2. Answers will vary.
3. He agreed to work with them if they worked towards achieving Confederation.
4. He designed the plan for the federal-provincial system we have today.
5. Answers will vary.

Sir Adams George Archibald: *(page 17)*
1. He was the financial advisor at the delegations so he could defend Confederation against the allegations of the anti-Confederates.
2. He established the basis for the civil institutions of Manitoba and the Northwest Territories and he negotiated the first two treaties with the natives.
3. He left his law practice and entered politics to help the province attain responsible government.
4. He was bilingual and was from the Maritimes. These qualities meant that he would be able to communicate with the people and he would not be biased in favour of any one group.

Campbell and Carter: *(page 21)*
1. Answers will vary.
2. He was there only as an observer from Newfoundland.
3. The people did not vote for Confederation because they had been told by the merchants that there would be higher taxes, and in 1869, they believed they would be better off on their own.
4. At that time, the French Shore Question of the fishing rights and land was a much more pressing issue.

Cartier and Chandler: *(page 24)*
1. The voters trusted him when he said that he believed that French Canada could better protect its distinct culture within Confederation.
2. It is ironic because he was part of the militia that fought against the government in the Rebellion of 1837.
3. He went to Canada to secure an agreement for building the railway and when guaranteed loans could not be found he went ahead with it anyway.
4. He handled such details as the sale of Rupert's Land to the government, the building of the Canadian Pacific and Grand Trunk Railways, and ending the siegneurial system in Quebec.

5. It was Cartier who gave the contract to Sir Hugh Allan and received money towards his campaign. This was seen as a bribe.

Chapais and Coles: *(page 27)*
1. He attended the conference as Commissioner of Public Works in the coalition government.
2. He established the Intercolonial Railway and developed the Grand Trunk Railway as well as helping to end the seigneurial system. He also passed the first Order in Council prohibiting American cattle from being imported into Canada.
3. He held a seat in the provincial Legislature and was also elected to the federal House of Commons.
4. He changed his mind when the offer to purchase foreign owned land holdings on Prince Edward Island was made part of the discussions at the Quebec Conference.
5. He refused to retract a statement he made in the Assembly.

Cockburn, Dickey and Fisher: *(page 30)*
1. Answers will vary.
2. He had to maintain a peaceful atmosphere between two enemies, John A. Macdonald and George Brown, and keep Thomas D'Arcy McGee from monopolizing the speeches.
3. The speeches he heard at the Charlottetown Conference convinced him that Confederation would not be a good thing for Nova Scotia.
4. They were not acceptable because the people of New Brunswick were satisfied with their present system of government.
5. Answers will vary.

Sir Alexander T. Galt: *(page 32)*
1. He came to Canada as a clerk with the British American Land Company.
2. The company was responsible for getting people to emigrate to Canada and settle there.
3. He thought that this was the only way to preserve the Anglo-Saxon Protestant way of life.
4. He was responsible for arranging the financial affairs of the new country.
5. He designed the Canadian currency of dollars and cents.

Gray, Gray, and Haviland: *(page 36)*
1. He did not make careful arrangements for the delegates and as a result there were no accommodations booked for them.
2. The people of Prince Edward Island had little interest in joining the other colonies. They did not have any hope that a town on the Island would be chosen to be the capital of the new nation and they feared they would lose their Legislature as a result of Confederation. They did not want to be part of the railway debts which had accumulated in the other colonies. In 1873, the Island was nearly bankrupt and had to join Confederation.
3. He had the reputation of wavering in his opinions.
4. He defended the Chinese and did authoritative work on the Canada - United States boundary disputes.
5. He grew up in a political atmosphere as his father was a politician.

Henry, Howland and Johnson: *(page 39)*
1. He was convinced that through Confederation, Nova Scotia would obtain a railway and free trade.
2. He objected to the limited number of Senators and the division of federal and provincial powers.
3. A clause was inserted in the British North America Act permitting the appointment of additional Senators on the recommendation of the Governor General.
4. He suggested that Senators be elected for a fixed term.
5. He served in various portfolios under Charles Fisher.

Langevin, MacDonald, and McCully: *(page 42)*
1. His opinions about the need for a strong federal government gave rise to provincial rights movements, particularly the Separatist movement.
2. He was the editor of a newspaper instead of working as a lawyer.
3. He thought there should be a larger number of Senators from the Maritimes.
4. He wrote editorials supporting Confederation in the newspapers.
5. He had a policy of cutting costs rather than concentrating on the government being efficient.

William McDougall: *(page 44)*
1. The aims were political institutions, suffrage for everyone, free trade with the United States, secularization of the clergy and representation by population.
2. His nickname was "Wandering Willie" because he changed political parties.
3. He called for the election of Senators rather than appointment.
4. He was instrumental in the purchase of Rupert's Land from the Hudson's Bay Company.
5. Louis Riel would not allow him to enter the territory.
6. He could only speak English so he would not be able to communicate with the people.

Thomas D'Arcy McGee: *(page 46)*
1. He constantly wrote about the concerns of the Irish people in Canada.
2. He supported Confederation and made speeches about it wherever he went.
3. It was a diplomatic tour of the Maritimes by politicians from Canada.
4. Answers will vary.

Mitchell and Mowat: *(page 49)*
1. He could discuss the financial aspects of Confederation with the voters.
2. He insisted that the railway follow the Gulf of St. Lawrence instead of taking an inland route.
3. Once he refused to approve estimates for the railway until a widow had been paid for a cow that had been struck by a train.
4. He developed the system of voting by using a ballot.
5. He was responsible for the provincial legislatures having the power to act on matters that concerned them.

Edward Palmer: *(page 51)*
1. He wanted everything to stay the same. He was against responsible government, against union with British North America and land reform.
2. He did not agree with the terms of union that were offered to Prince Edward Island.
3. He switched parties because the Liberals were against Confederation.
4. The debt of the railway and the fact that Prince Edward Island was almost bankrupt changed his mind about Confederation.

William Henry Pope: *(page 53)*
1. At that time, the government was experimenting with nondepartmentalism - a practice of having civil servants head the various government departments.
2. He believed that property rights had to be respected and that the Imperial government was responsible for the problem.
3. He was one of a few Conservatives that supported Confederation.
4. He wrote letters, gave lectures, and tried to rebuild the party into a pro-Confederation party.

Ritchie and Shea: *(page 56)*
1. It was a committee that met to discuss colonial trade. It recommended that the colonies take joint action in commercial policies, send trade missions to the West Indies and South America and that one of its members should act with the British minister on trade negotiations in Washington.
2. He hoped that by joining Confederation Newfoundlanders would benefit financially.
3. The merchants told the people that Confederation would mean higher taxes and prices and other dreadful economic results
4. He hoped to get Newfoundlanders to work on the construction. The result was that many of the people who were hired left and those that stayed never returned to Newfoundland.
5. Answers will vary.

Steeves and Tache: *(page 59)*
1. Answers will vary.
2. Answers will vary.
3. He was called out of retirement because he was known as an impartial person who would form a government that would work, and not just form one made up of his friends.
4. He gave a speech on the need for Lower Canada to have a militia.
5. Answers will vary.

Tilley and Tupper: *(page 63)*
1. He was reading the Bible and came across Psalm 72 which says "He shall have Dominion from sea to sea... ."
2. The area now known as Canada stretches from sea to sea.
3. He planned a meeting at Charlottetown to discuss a union of the Maritime colonies.
4. He oversaw the completion of the Canadian Pacific Railway, the Welland Canal, and other small railway lines.
5. He was called back to fight the election against Fielding, who wanted to take Nova Scotia out of Confederation.

Whelan and Wilmot: *(page 66)*
1. He used his newspaper to fight for responsible government.
2. The people who supported his ideas were the poor.
3. He saw Confederation as a way to free the Island from the control of the Colonial Office and to solve the Absentee Landlord's Question.
4. He thought that too much power was being given to the federal government.
5. When he attended a meeting of the Confederate Council on Commercial Treaties, he realized that Canada East would never accept a legislative union. If there was to be Confederation, it would have to have a federal government.

Who were they?: *(page 67-69)*

Adams Archibald	Nova Scotia	doctor
George Brown	Canada	newspaper editor
Alexander Campbell	Canada	lawyer
Frederic Carter	Newfoundland	lawyer
George-Étienne Cartier	Canada	lawyer
Edward Chandler	New Brunswick	lawyer
Jean-Charles Chapais	Canada	merchant
James Cockburn	Canada	lawyer
George Coles	Prince Edward Island	merchant
Robert Dickey	Nova Scotia	lawyer
Charles Fisher	New Brunswick	lawyer
Alexander Galt	Canada	clerk
John Hamilton Gray	Prince Edward Island	cavalry officer
John Hamilton Gray	New Brunswick	lawyer
William Henry	Nova Scotia	lawyer
William Howland	Canada	merchant
John Johnson	New Brunswick	lawyer
Hector-Louis Langevin	Canada	journalist, lawyer
Jonathan McCully	Nova Scotia	lawyer

Who Were They?: *(cont'd)*

A.A. MacDonald	Prince Edward Island	merchant, shipowner
John A. Macdonald	Canada	lawyer
William McDougall	Canada	lawyer
Thomas D'Arcy McGee	Canada	newspaper editor
Peter Mitchell	New Brunswick	lawyer
Oliver Mowat	Canada	lawyer
Edward Palmer	Prince Edward Island	lawyer
William Pope	Prince Edward Island	lawyer, land agent
John Ritchie	Nova Scotia	lawyer
Ambrose Shea	Newfoundland	merchant
William Steeves	New Brunswick	merchant
Etienne - Paschal Tache	Canada	doctor
Leonard Tilley	New Brunswick	pharmacist
Charles Tupper	Nova Scotia	doctor
Edward Whelan	Prince Edward Island	printer
R.D. Wilmot	New Brunswick	merchant

Quiz 1: *(page 71-70)*

1. It refers to the men who attended the conferences to discuss Confederation.
2. It was taken from the Bible by Sir Samuel Leonard Tilley.
3. They were held at Charlottetown, Quebec and London.
4. The four provinces that joined Confederation in 1867 were Nova Scotia, New Brunswick, Quebec and Ontario.
5. It was the law that officially created the country of Canada.
6. It was a document drawn up at the Quebec Conference which set out how the new country was to be governed. It is sometimes called the Quebec Resolutions because it was developed at Quebec.
7. They were afraid they would not gain anything from the union.
8. They were afraid that the Americans would try to annex Canada, treaties with the United States were not renewed, Britain began to trade with other countries, and the government of the Province of Canada was not working.
9. It meant that the number of representatives in government should be related to the population of the province. It was developed by George Brown.
10. He developed the constitution which governed the new nation.

Quiz 2: *(page 73)*

Part A

1. i   2. h   3. g   4. f   5. a   6. j   7. b   8. c   9. d   10. e

Part B

1. Father of Confederation   2. Smasher   3. The Little Nun   4. The Grand Old Man   5. Wandering Willie

Page 75:

1. true   2. false   3. false   4. true   5. false   6. true   7. true   8. true   9. false   10. true
11. false   12. true   13. false   14. true   15. true